WEB

WEB to cweb

Converting TEX from WEB to cweb

Für meinen Vater

MARTIN RUCKERT *Munich University of Applied Sciences*

Date: 2017-08-30 16:46:23 +0200 (Wed, 30 Aug 2017)

Revision: 999

The author has taken care in the preparation of this book, but makes no expressed or implied warranty of any kind and assumes no responsibility for errors or omissions. No liability is assumed for incidental or consequential damages in connection with or arising out of the use of the information or programs contained herein.

```
Ruckert, Martin.
WEB to cweb
Includes index.
ISBN 1-548-58234-4
```

Internet page https://w3-o.cs.hm.edu/~ruckert/web2w/ may contain current information about this book, downloadable software, and news.

Copyright © 2017 by Martin Ruckert

All rights reserved. Printed using CreateSpace. This publication is protected by copyright, and permission must be obtained from the publisher prior to any prohibited reproduction, storage in a retrieval system, or transmission in any form or by any means, electronic, mechanical, photocopying, recording, or likewise. To obtain permission to use material from this work, please submit a written request to Martin Ruckert, Hochschule München, Fakultät für Informatik und Mathematik, Lothstrasse 64, 80335 München, Germany.

ruckert@cs.hm.edu

ISBN-10: 1-548-58234-4
ISBN-13: 987-1548582340

First printing, August 2017

Preface

This book describes a project to convert the TeX source code[5] written by Donald E. Knuth as a "WEB"[6] into a "cweb"[2].

- On December 9, 2016, I started to implement web2w as a compiler for WEB files which is described below. The compiler, as compilers usually do, reads an input file and continues to produce a parse tree. The resulting parse tree has two structures: a linear structure representing the linear order of the input file and a tree structure representing the embedded Pascal program. Then the embedded Pascal program needs to be translated into an equivalent C program. And finally, the linear structure of the parse tree will be used to output a cweb file. Small corrections on the resulting cweb file are implemented by a patch file.

  The overall goal is the generation of a ctex.w file that is as close as possible to the tex.web input file, and can be used to produce ctex.tex and ctex.c using the standard tools ctangle and cweave.

  The TeX program can then be compiled from ctex.c and the TeX documentation can be generated from ctex.tex by TeX itself.

  This will simplify the tool chain necessary to generate TeX from its "sources".

- On April 20, 2017, I was able to create the first "hello world" dvi file with my newly generated TeX program and with that, I had reached version 0.1 of web2w.

- On April 26, 2017, I succeeded for the first time to generate a program that would pass the trip test and therefore can be called TeX. This was then version 0.2 of web2w.

  While the program at this point was a "correct implementation of TeX", its form still needed further improvement. For example, the sizes of arrays were computed and occurred in the source as literal numbers. It would be appropriate for source code that instead the expression defining the array size were used to specify the array size. The use of **return** statements and the elimination of unused *end* labels also asked for improvement.

- On May 11, 2017, I completed version 0.3 of web2w. Numerous improvements were added by then: some concerning the presentation of web2w itself, others with the goal of generating better cweb code for TeX. I decided then to freeze the improvement of the code for a while and prepare this document for publication as a book.

- On July 27, 2017, I completed version 0.4 of web2w, the first version that will be published as a book. More improvements (and more versions) are still to come.

Of course, changes in the code part of TeX will necessarily require changes in the documentation part. These can, however, not result from an automatic compilation. So the plan is to develop patch files that generate from the latest $0.x$ versions improved $1.y$ versions. These versions will share the same goal as version $0.x$: producing a `cweb` TeX source file that is as close as possible to the original web source but with a documentation part of each section that reflects the changes made in the code.

- There is a long term goal that brought me to construct `web2w` in the first place: I plan to derive from the TeX sources a new kind of TeX that is influenced by the means and necessities of current software and hardware. The name for this new implementation will be HINT which is, in the usual Open Software naming schema, the acronym for "HINT is not TeX".

  For example, HINT will accept UTF-8 input files because this is the defacto standard due to its use on the world wide web. Further, the machine model will be a processor that can efficiently handle 64-Bit values and has access to large amounts of main memory (several GByte). Last not least, I assume the availability of a good modern C compiler and will leave optimizations to the compiler if possible.

  The major change however will be the separation of the TeX frontend: the processing of `.tex` files, from the TeX backend: the rendering of paragraphs and pages.

  Let's look, for example, at ebooks: Current ebooks are of minor typographic quality. Just compiling TeX sources to a standard ebook format, for example epub, does not work because a lot of information that is used by TeX to produce good looking pages is not available in these formats. So I need to cut TeX (or HINT) in two pieces: a frontend, that reads TeX input and a backend that renders pixel on a page. The frontend will not know about the final page size because the size of the output medium may change while we read—for example by turning a mobile device from landscape to portrait mode. On the other hand, the computational resources of the backend are usually limited because a mobile device has a limited supply of electrical energy. So we should do as much as we can in the frontend and postpone what needs to be postponed to the backend. In between front and back, we need a nice new file format, that is compact and efficient, and transports whatever information is necessary between both parts.

  These are the possible next steps:

- As a first step, I will make a version of TeX that produces a file listing all the contributions and insertions that TeX sends to the page builder. Let's call this a `.hint` file. This version of TeX will become the final frontend.

- Next, I will use a second version of TeX where I replace the reading of `.tex` files by the reading of a `.hint` file and feeding its content directly to the page builder. This version of TeX will become the final backend. Once done, I can test the equation TeX = HINT frontend + HINT backend.

- Next, I will replace the generation of dvi files in the backend by directly displaying the results in a "viewer". The "viewer" reads in a `.hint` file and

uses it to display one single page at an arbitrary position. Using page up and page down buttons, the viewer can be used to navigate in the .hint file. At that point, it should be possible to change `vsize` dynamically in the viewer.
- The hardest part will be the removal of `hsize` dependencies from the frontend and moving them to the backend. I am still not sure how this will work out.
- Once the author of a TeX document can no longer specify the final `hsize` and `vsize`, he or she would probably wish to be able to write conditional text for different ranges of `hsize` and `vsize`. So if the frontend encounters such tests it needs to include all variants in its output file.
- Last not least, most people use LaTeX not plain TeX. Hence, if I want many people to use HINT, it should be able to work with LaTeX. As a first step, I looked at ε-TeX, and my cweb version of ε-TeX already passes the extended trip test for ε-TeX. But I am not sure what LaTeX needs beside the extensions of ε-TeX. So if someone knows, please let me know.

Enough now of these fussy ideas about the future. Let's turn to the present and the conversion of TeX from WEB to cweb.

San Luis Obispo, CA
June 27, 2017   *Martin Ruckert*

Contents

	Preface	v
	Contents	ix
	List of Figures and Tables	xi
1	**Introduction**	**1**
2	**Converting WEB to cweb**	**7**
3	**Reading the WEB**	**9**
	3.1 Scanning the WEB	9
	3.2 Tokens	10
	3.3 Scanner actions	13
	3.4 Strings	13
	3.5 Identifiers	15
	3.6 Linking related tokens	18
	3.7 Module names	20
	3.8 Definitions	22
	3.9 Finishing the token list	23
4	**Parsing Pascal**	**25**
	4.1 Generating the sequence of Pascal tokens	25
	4.2 Simple cases for the parser	27
	4.3 The macros **debug**, **gubed**, and friends	28
	4.4 Parsing numerical constants	30
	4.5 Expanding module names and macros	31
	4.6 Expanding macros with parameters	32
	4.7 The function *ppparse*	33
5	**Writing the cweb**	**35**
	5.1 cweb output routines	35
	5.2 Traversing the WEB	36
	5.3 Simple cases of conversion	37
	5.4 Pascal division	39
	5.5 Identifiers	40
	5.6 Strings	41
	5.7 Module names	42
	5.8 Replacing the WEB string pool file	42
	5.9 Macro and format declarations	48
	5.10 Labels	50

	5.11	Constant declarations	52
	5.12	Variable declarations	52
	5.13	Types	53
	5.14	Files	57
	5.15	Structured statements	57
	5.16	**for**-loops	60
	5.17	Semicolons	63
	5.18	Procedures	66
	5.19	Functions	68
	5.20	The *main* program	71
6	Predefined symbols in Pascal		73
7	Processing the command line		75
8	Error handling and debugging		79
9	The scanner		81
10	The parser		87
11	Generating TeX, Running TeX, and Passing the Trip Test		105
	11.1	Generating TeX	105
	11.2	Running TeX	106
	11.3	Passing the Trip Test	109
	11.4	Generating `ctex.w` from `tex.web`	109
	References		111
	Index		113
	Crossreference of Sections		125

List of Figures and Tables

Figures

Fig. 1: WEB code for *new_null_box* 2
Fig. 2: cweb code for *new_null_box* 2
Fig. 3: The C code for *new_null_box* as generated by web2c 2
Fig. 4: The WEB code for *new_character* 3
Fig. 5: The cweb code for *new_character* 3

Tables

Tab. 1: List of linked tokens 18

1 Introduction

web2w, the program that follows, was not written following an established software engineering workflow as we teach it in our software engineering classes. Instead the development of this program was driven by an ongoing exploration of the problem at hand where the daily dose of success or failure would determine the direction I would go on the next day.

This description of my program development approach sounds a bit like "rapid prototyping". But "prototype" implies the future existence of a "final" version and I do not intend to produce such a "final" version. Actually I have no intention to finish the prototype either, and I might change it in the future in unpredictable ways. I expect, however, that the speed of its further development will certainly decrease as I move on to other problems. Instead I have documented the development process as a literate program: the pages you are just reading. So in terms of literature, this is not an epic novel with a carefully designed plot, but it's more like the diary of an explorer who sets out to travel trough yet uncharted territories.

The territory ahead of me was the program TEX written by Donald E. Knuth using the WEB language as a literate program. As such, it contains snippets of code in the programming language Pascal—Pascal-H to be precise. Pascal-H is Charles Hedrick's modification of a compiler for the DECsystem-10 that was originally developed at the University of Hamburg (cf. [3] see [5]). So I could not expect to find a pure "Standard Pascal". But then, the implementation of TEX deliberately does not use the full set of features that the language Pascal has to offer in order to make it easier to run TEX on a large variety of machines. At the beginning, it was unclear to me what problems I would encounter with the subset of Pascal that is actually used in TEX.

Further, the problem was not the translation of Pascal to C. A program that does this is available in the TEX Live project: web2c[1] translates the Pascal code that is produced using **tangle** from **tex.web** into C code. The C code that is generated this way can, however, not be regarded as human readable source code. The following example might illustrate this: Figure 1 shows the WEB code for the function *new_null_box*. The result of translating it to C by web2c can be seen in figure 3. In contrast, figure 2 shows what web2w will achieve.

It can be seen, that web2c has desugared the sweet code written by Knuth to make it unpalatable to human beings, the only use you can make of it is feeding it to a C compiler. In contrast, web2w tries to create source code that is as close to the original as possible but still translates Pascal to C. For example, note the last statement in the *new_null_box* function: where C has a **return** statement, Pascal

136. The *new_null_box* function returns a pointer to an *hlist_node* in which all subfields have the values corresponding to '\hbox{}'. The *subtype* field is set to *min_quarterword*, since that's the desired *span_count* value if this *hlist_node* is changed to an *unset_node*.

function *new_null_box*: *pointer*;
　　　{ creates a new box node }
　var *p*: *pointer*;　{ the new node }
　begin $p \leftarrow get\_node(box\_node\_size)$;
　$type(p) \leftarrow hlist\_node$;
　$subtype(p) \leftarrow min\_quarterword$;
　$width(p) \leftarrow 0$;　$depth(p) \leftarrow 0$;
　$height(p) \leftarrow 0$;　$shift\_amount(p) \leftarrow 0$;
　$list\_ptr(p) \leftarrow null$;
　$glue\_sign(p) \leftarrow normal$;
　$glue\_order(p) \leftarrow normal$;
　$set\_glue\_ratio\_zero(glue\_set(p))$;
　$new\_null\_box \leftarrow p$;
　end;

Fig. 1: WEB *code for new_null_box*

136. The *new_null_box* function returns a pointer to an *hlist_node* in which all subfields have the values corresponding to '\hbox{}'. The *subtype* field is set to *min_quarterword*, since that's the desired *span_count* value if this *hlist_node* is changed to an *unset_node*.

pointer *new_null_box*(**void**)
　/∗ creates a new box node ∗/
　{ **pointer** *p*;　　/∗ the new node ∗/
　$p = get\_node(box\_node\_size)$;
　$type(p) = hlist\_node$;
　$subtype(p) = min\_quarterword$;
　$width(p) = 0$;　$depth(p) = 0$;
　$height(p) = 0$;　$shift\_amount(p) = 0$;
　$list\_ptr(p) = null$;
　$glue\_sign(p) = normal$;
　$glue\_order(p) = normal$;
　$set\_glue\_ratio\_zero(glue\_set(p))$;
　return *p*;
　}

Fig. 2: cweb *code for new_null_box*

```
halfword
newnullbox ( void )
{
  register halfword Result; newnullbox_regmem
  halfword p ;
  p = getnode ( 7 ) ;
  mem [p ].hh.b0 = 0 ;
  mem [p ].hh.b1 = 0 ;
  mem [p + 1 ].cint = 0 ;
  mem [p + 2 ].cint = 0 ;
  mem [p + 3 ].cint = 0 ;
  mem [p + 4 ].cint = 0 ;
  mem [p + 5 ].hh .v.RH = -268435455L ;
  mem [p + 5 ].hh.b0 = 0 ;
  mem [p + 5 ].hh.b1 = 0 ;
  mem [p + 6 ].gr = 0.0 ;
  Result = p ;
  return Result ;
}
```

Fig. 3: *The C code for new_null_box as generated by* web2c

assigns the return value to the function name. A simple translation, sufficient for a C compiler, can just replace the function name by "`Result`" (an identifier that is not used in the implementation of TeX) and add "`return Result;`" at the end of the function (see figure 3). A translation that strives to produce nice code should, however, avoid such ugly code.

Let's look at another example:

function *new_character*(*f* : *internal_font_number*; *c* : *eight_bits*): *pointer*;
   label *exit*;
   var *p*: *pointer*;   { newly allocated node }
   begin if *font_bc*[*f*] ≤ *c* **then**
     if *font_ec*[*f*] ≥ *c* **then**
       if *char_exists*(*char_info*(*f*)(*qi*(*c*))) **then**
         begin *p* ← *get_avail*; *font*(*p*) ← *f*; *character*(*p*) ← *qi*(*c*);
         new_character ← *p*; **return**;
         end;
   char_warning(*f*, *c*); *new_character* ← *null*;
exit: **end**;

Fig. 4: The `WEB` code for *new_character*

pointer *new_character*(**internal_font_number** *f*, **eight_bits** *c*)
{ **pointer** *p*;   /* newly allocated node */
   if (*font_bc*[*f*] ≤ *c*)
     if (*font_ec*[*f*] ≥ *c*)
       if (*char_exists*(*char_info*(*f*)(*qi*(*c*)))) { *p* = *get_avail*(); *font*(*p*) = *f*;
         character(*p*) = *qi*(*c*); **return** *p*;
       }
   char_warning(*f*, *c*); **return** *null*;
}

Fig. 5: The `cweb` code for *new_character*

In figure 4 there is a "**return**" in the innermost **if**. This "**return**" is actually a macro defined as "**goto** *exit*", and "*exit*" is a numeric macro defined as "10". "return" is a reserved word in C and "exit" is a function of the C standard library, so something has to be done. The example also illustrates the point that I can not always replace an assignment to the function name by a C return statement. Only if the assignment is in a tail position, that is a position where the control-flow leads directly to the end of the function body, it can be turned into a return statement as happened in figure 5. Further, if all the goto statements that lead to a given label have been eliminated, as it is the case here, the label can be eliminated as well. In figure 5 there is no "*exit*:" preceding the final "}".

Another seemingly small problem is the different use of semicolons in C and Pascal. While in C a semicolon follows an expression to make it into a statement, in Pascal the semicolon connects two statements into a statement sequence. For example, if an assignment precedes an "**else**", in Pascal you have "`x:=0 else`" where as in C you have "`x=0; else`"; no additional semicolon is needed if a compound statement precedes the "**else**". When converting `tex.web`, a total of 1119 semicolons need to be inserted at the right places. Speaking of the right place: Consider the following WEB code:

if $s \geq \mathit{str\_ptr}$ **then** $s \leftarrow$ "???" { this can't happen }
else if $s < 256$ **then**

Where should the semicolon go? Directly preceding the "**else**"? Probably not! Alternatively, I can start the search for the right place to insert the semicolon with the assignment. But this does not work either: the assignment can be spread over several macros or modules which can be used multiple times; so the right place to insert a semicolon in one instance can be the wrong place in another instance. `web2w` places the semicolon correctly behind the assignment like this:

if $(s \geq \mathit{str\_ptr})$ $s = \langle$ "???" 1381 $\rangle$; /∗ this can't happen ∗/
else if $(s < 256)$

But look what happened to the string `"???"`. Strings enclosed in C-like double quotes receive a special treatment by `tangle`: the strings are collected in a string pool file and replaced by string numbers in the Pascal source. No such mechanism is available in `ctangle`. My first attempt was to replace the string handling of TEX and keep the C-like strings in the source code. TEXs string pool is, however, hardwired into the program and is used not only for static strings but also for strings created at runtime, for example the names of control sequences. So I tried a hybrid approach: keeping strings that are used only for output (error messages for example) and translating other strings to string numbers. There are different places where the translation of a string like `"Maybe␣you␣should␣try␣asking␣a␣human?"` to a number like 283 can take place.

1. One could add a function s to do the translation at runtime and then write $s($`"Maybe␣you␣should␣try␣asking␣a␣human?"`$)$. The advantage is simplicity and readability; the disadvantage is the overhead in time and space (the string will exist twice: as a static string and as a copy in the string pool).

2. One could use the C preprocessor to do the job. For example, I could generate a macro *Maybe_you_should_try_asking_a_human0x63* that is defined as 283 and a second macro *str_283* for the string itself. Then, I can replace the occurrence of the string in the source by the macro name that mimics the string content and initialize the *str_pool* and *str_start* array using the other macro.

3. As a third variation used below, one can use the module expansion mechanism of `ctangle`. I generate for each string a module, in the above example named $\langle$ `"Maybe␣you␣should␣try␣asking␣a␣human?"` 1234 $\rangle$, that will expand to the correct number, here 283. And as in the previous method use a macro *str_283* to initialize *str_pool* and *str_start*. The advantage is the greater flexibility and the nicer looking replacements for strings, because module names can use the full character set. (Imagine replacing `"???"` by *_0x630x630x63*.)

In retrospect, after seeing how nice method 3 works, I ponder if I should have decided to avoid the hybrid approach and use approach 3 for all strings. It would

1 Introduction

have reduced the amount of changes to the source file considerably. I further think that approach 1 has its merits too. The overhead in space is just a few thousand byte and the overhead in time is incurred only when the strings are actually needed which is mostly during a run of `initex` and while generating output (which is slow anyway).

A mayor difference between Pascal and C is the use of subrange types. Subrange types are used to specify the range of valid indices when defining arrays. While most arrays used in TEX start with index zero, not all do. In the first case, they can be implemented as C arrays which always start at index zero; in the latter case, I define a zero based array having the right size, adding a "0" to the name. Then, I define a constant pointer initialized by the address of the zero based array plus/minus a suitable offset so that I can use this pointer as a replacement for the Pascal array.

When subrange types are used to define variables, I replace subrange types by the next largest C standard integer type as defined in `stdint.h` which works most of the time. Consider the code

    var p: $0 \mathinner{\ldotp\ldotp} \mathit{nest\_size}$;   { index into nest }

    $\vdots$

    for $p \leftarrow \mathit{nest\_ptr}$ **downto** 0 **do**

where $\mathit{nest\_size} = 40$. Translating this to

    uint8_t p;   /* index into nest */

    $\vdots$

    for $(p = \mathit{nest\_ptr};\ p \geq 0;\ p\mathord{-}\mathord{-})$

would result in an infinite loop because p would never become less than zero; instead it would wrap around. So in this (and 21 similar cases), I declare the variables used in for-loops to be of type **int**.

I will not go into further details of the translation process as you will find all the information in what follows below. Instead, I will take a step back now and give you the big picture, looking back at the journey that took me to this point.

The program `web2w` works in three phases: First I run the input file `tex.web` through a scanner producing tokens (see section 9). The pattern matching is done using `flex`, the action code consists of macros described here. The tokens form a doubly linked list, so that later I can traverse the source file forward and backward. During scanning, information is gathered and stored about macros, identifiers, and modules. In addition, every token has a *link* field which is used to connect related tokens. For example, I link an opening parenthesis to the matching closing parenthesis, and the start of a comment to the end of the comment.

After scanning comes parsing. The parser is generated using `bison` from a modified Pascal grammar (see section 10). To run the parser, I need to feed it with tokens, rearranged in the order that `tangle` would produce, expanding macros and modules as I go. While parsing, I gather information about the Pascal code. At the beginning, I tended to use this information immediately to rearrange the token sequence just parsed. Later, I learned the hard way (modules that were modified on the first encounter would later be feed to the parser in the modified form) that it is better to leave the token sequence untouched and just annotate it with information needed to transform it during the next stage. A technique that proved to be very useful is connecting the key tokens of a Pascal structure using the *link* field. For example, connecting a "**case**" token with its "**do**" token makes it easy to place the expression that is between these tokens, without knowing anything about its actual structure, between " **switch** (" and ")". The final stage is the generation of `cweb` output. Here the token sequence is traversed a third time, this time again in input file order. This time, the traversal will stop at the warning signs put up during the first two passes, use the information gathered so far, and rewrite the token sequence as gentle and respectful as possible from Pascal to C.

Et voilà! `tex.w` is ready—almost at least. I apply a last patch file, for instance to adapt documentation reliant on `webmac.tex` so that it works with `cwebmac.tex`, or I make small changes that do not deserve a more general treatment. The final file is then called `ctex.w` from which I obtain `ctex.c` and `ctex.tex` simply by applying `ctangle` and `cweave`. Using "`gcc ctex.c -o ctex`" I get a running `ctex`. Running "`ctex ctex.tex`" to get `ctex.dvi` is then just a tiny step away: it is necessary to set up format and font metric files. The details on how to do that and run (and pass) the infamous trip test are described in section 11.

2 Converting WEB to cweb

web2w is implemented by a C code file:

#include <stdlib.h> (1)
#include <stdio.h>
#include <ctype.h>
#include <string.h>
#include <stdbool.h>
#include <stdint.h>
#include <math.h>
#include "web2w.h"
#include "pascal.tab.h"
  ⟨ internal declarations 3 ⟩
  ⟨ global variables 11 ⟩
  ⟨ functions 13 ⟩
  int $main$(int $argc$, char $*argv$[ ])
  {
    ⟨ process the command line 213 ⟩
    ⟨ read the WEB 4 ⟩
    ⟨ parse Pascal 92 ⟩
    ⟨ generate cweb output 100 ⟩
    ⟨ show summary 12 ⟩
    return 0;
  }

I also create the header file web2w.h included in the above C file. It contains the external declarations and is used to share constants, macros, types, variables, and functions with other C files.

⟨ web2w.h 2 ⟩ ≡ (2)
  ⟨ external declarations 5 ⟩

3 Reading the WEB

When I read the WEB, I split it into a list of tokens; this process is called "scanning". I use **flex** (the free counterpart of **lex**) to generate the function *wwlex* from the file **web.l**.

⟨ internal declarations 3 ⟩ ≡   (3)
   extern int *wwlex*(**void**);   /∗ the scanner ∗/
   extern FILE ∗*wwin*;   /∗ the scanners input file ∗/
   extern FILE ∗*wwout*;   /∗ the scanners needs an output file ∗/

Used in 1.

Using this function, I can read the WEB and produce a token list.

⟨ read the WEB 4 ⟩ ≡   (4)
   ⟨ initialize token list 22 ⟩
   wwlex( ); ⟨ finalize token list 66 ⟩   Used in 1.

Reading the WEB results in a list of tokens as used by **tangle** or **weave**. At this point, I do not need to extract the structure of the Pascal program contained in the WEB. This is left for a later stage. I need to extract the WEB specific structure: text in limbo followed by modules; modules starting with TEX text followed optionally by definitions and Pascal code. Aside from this general structure, I will later need to translate the WEB specific control sequences (starting with @) by **cweb** specific control sequences.

The scanner identifies tokens by matching the input against regular expressions and executing C code if a match is found. The lex file **web.l** is not a literate program since it's not a C file; it is given verbatim in section 9. The functions and macros used in the action parts inside the file, however, are described below.

3.1 Scanning the WEB

The scanner is written following the WEB User Manual[4].

It has three main modes: the INITIAL mode (or TEX mode), the MIDDLE mode, and the PASCAL mode; and three special modes DEFINITION, FORMAT, and NAME.

⟨ external declarations 5 ⟩ ≡   (5)
#**define** TEX   INITIAL   Used in 2.

The scanner starts out in TEX mode scanning the part of the file that is "in limbo" and then switches back and forth between TEX mode, MIDDLE mode, and PASCAL mode, occasionally taking a detour through DEFINITION, FORMAT, or NAME mode.

While scanning in TEX mode, I need to deal with a few special characters: the character "@", because it introduces special web commands and might introduce a change into Pascal mode; the "|" character, because it starts Pascal mode; and the "{" and "}" characters, which are used for grouping while in TEX mode. Unfortunately, these same characters also start and end comments while in Pascal mode. So finding a "}" in TEX mode might be the end of a group or the end of a comment. Everything else is just considered plain text. Text may also contain the "@", "|", "{", and "}" characters if these are preceded by a backslash.

In PASCAL mode, I match the tokens needed to build the Pascal parse tree. These are different—and far more numerous—than what I need for the TEX part which my translator will not touch at all. The MIDDLE mode is a restricted PASCAL mode that does not allow module names. Instead, a module name terminates MIDDLE mode and starts a new module.

The DEFINITION mode is used to scan the initial part of a macro definition; the FORMAT mode is a simplified version of the DEFINITION mode used for format definitions; and the NAME mode is used to scan module names.

In PASCAL mode, I ignore most spaces and match the usual Pascal tokens. The main work is left to the Pascal parser.

The switching between the scanning modes is supported by a stack (see section 3.6) because it may involve nested structures. For example inside Pascal, a comment contains TEX code and inside TEX code whatever comes between two "|" characters is considered Pascal code. A scanner produced by flex is very fast, but by itself not capable of tracking nested structures.

3.2 Tokens

The parser creates a representation of the WEB file as a list of tokens. Later the parser will build a parse tree with tokens as leaf nodes. Because C lacks object orientation, I define **token** as a **union** of leaf nodes and internal nodes of the tree. All instances of the type defined this way share a common *tag* field as a replacement for the class information. Every token has a pointer to the *next* token, a pointer the *previous* token, a *link* field to connect related tokens, and an *up* pointer pointing from the leafs upwards and from internal nodes upwards until reaching the root node.

⟨ external declarations 5 ⟩ +≡ (6)
  typedef struct token {
    int *tag*;
    struct token ∗*next*, ∗*previous*, ∗*link*, ∗*up*;
    union {
      ⟨ leaf node 7 ⟩;
      ⟨ internal node 93 ⟩;
    };
  } **token**;

Leaf nodes also contain a sequence number, enumerating stretches of contiguous Pascal code, and for debugging purposes, a line number field. There is some more token specific information, that will be explained as needed.

3.2 Tokens

⟨ leaf node 7 ⟩ ≡ (7)
  struct {
    int *sequenceno*;
    int *lineno*;
    ⟨ token specific info 8 ⟩
  }
                                                                      Used in 6.

As a first example for token specific information, I note that most tokens have a *text* field that contains the textual representation of the token.

⟨ token specific info 8 ⟩ ≡ (8)
  char *∗text*;
                                                                        Used in 7.

The assignment of the *tag* numbers is mostly arbitrary. The file `pascal.y` lists all possible tags and gives them symbolic names which are shown using small caps in the following. The function *tagname*, defined in `pascal.y`, is responsible for converting the tag numbers back into readable strings.

⟨ external declarations 5 ⟩ += (9)
  extern const char *∗tagname*(**int** *tag*);

Because I do not deallocate tokens, I can simply allocate them from a token array using the function *new_token*.

⟨ internal declarations 3 ⟩ += (10)
#define `MAX_TOKEN_MEM` 250000

⟨ global variables 11 ⟩ ≡ (11)
  static token *token_mem*[`MAX_TOKEN_MEM`] = {{0}};
  static int *free_tokens* = `MAX_TOKEN_MEM`;
                                                      Used in 1.

⟨ show summary 12 ⟩ ≡ (12)
  `DBG`(*dbgbasic*, `"free tokens = %d\n"`, *free_tokens*);
                                           Used in 1.

⟨ functions 13 ⟩ ≡ (13)
  static token *∗new_token*(**int** *tag*)
  {
    token *∗n*;
    if (*free_tokens* > 0) *n* = &*token_mem*[−−*free_tokens*];
    else `ERROR`(`"token mem overflow"`);
    n→lineno = *wwlineno*; *n→sequenceno* = *sequenceno*; *n→tag* = *tag*;
    return *n*;
  }
                                                                 Used in 1.

The value of *wwlineno*, the current line number, is maintained automatically by the code generated from `web.l`.

⟨ external declarations 5 ⟩ += (14)
  extern int *wwlineno*;

The value of *sequenceno* is taken from a global variable.

⟨ global variables 11 ⟩ += (15)
  int *sequenceno* = 0;

I increment this variable as part of the scanner actions using the macro SEQ.

⟨ external declarations 5 ⟩ +≡ (16)
   extern int *sequenceno*;
#**define** SEQ (*sequenceno*++)

The following function is used in the parser to verify that two tokens t and s belong to the same token sequence.

⟨ external declarations 5 ⟩ +≡ (17)
   void *seq*(**token** *t, **token** *s);

⟨ functions 13 ⟩ +≡ (18)
   void *seq*(**token** *t, **token** *s)
   {
     CHECK($t{\rightarrow}sequenceno \equiv s{\rightarrow}sequenceno$,
       "tokens␣in␣line␣%d␣and␣%d␣belong␣to␣different␣code␣sequences",
       $t{\rightarrow}lineno, s{\rightarrow}lineno$);
   }

The list of tokens is created by the function *add_token*.

⟨ external declarations 5 ⟩ +≡ (19)
   extern token *add_token(**int** tag);

The function creates a new token and adds it to the global list of all tokens maintaining two pointers, one to the first and one to the last token of the list.

⟨ global variables 11 ⟩ +≡ (20)
   static token *$first\_token$;
   token *$last\_token$;

⟨ external declarations 5 ⟩ +≡ (21)
   extern token *$last\_token$;

I initialize the list of tokens by creating a HEAD token, and make it the first and last token of the list.

⟨ initialize token list 22 ⟩ ≡ (22)
   $first\_token = last\_token = new\_token$(HEAD); $first\_token{\rightarrow}text =$ ""; Used in 4.

⟨ functions 13 ⟩ +≡ (23)
   token *add_token(**int** tag)
   {
     token *$n = new\_token(tag)$;
     $last\_token{\rightarrow}next = n$; $n{\rightarrow}previous = last\_token$; $last\_token = n$; **return** n;
   }

3.3 Scanner actions

Now I am ready to explain scanner actions. Let's start with the most simple cases. There are quite a few tokens, that are just added to the token list and have a fixed literal string as textual representation. I use the macro TOK to do this. Making TOK an external declaration will write its definition into the file web2w.h which will be included by web.l.

⟨external declarations 5⟩ +≡ (24)
#define TOK(*string*, *tag*) (*add_token*(*tag*)→*text* = *string*)

Another class of simple tokens are those that have a varying textual representation which is defined by the string found in the input file. The variable *wwtext* points to this input string after it was matched against the regular expression. Since these strings are not persistent, I need to use the string handling function *copy_string* before I can store them in the tokens *text* field. The macro COPY can be used together with TOK to achieve the desired effect.

⟨external declarations 5⟩ +≡ (25)
#define COPY *copy_string*(*wwtext*)

The last class of tokens that I discuss before I turn my attention to the functions that actually do the string-handling are the tokens where the textual representation is build up in small increments. Three macros are used to perform the desired operations: BOS (Begin of String) is used to start a new string, ADD adds characters to the current string, and EOS (End of String) is used to complete the definition of the string.

⟨external declarations 5⟩ +≡ (26)
#define BOS *new_string*( )
#define ADD *add_string*(*wwtext*)
#define EOS (*string_length*( ) > 0 ? TOK(*end_string*( ), TEXT) : 0)

More string handling functions are used to define these macros and it is time to explain the string handling in more detail.

3.4 Strings

In this section, I define the following functions:

⟨external declarations 5⟩ +≡ (27)
  extern char **new_string*(**void**);   /* start a new string */
  extern void *add_string*(**char** **str*);   /* add characters to the string */
  extern char **end_string*(**void**);   /* finish the string */
  extern char **copy_string*(**char** **str*); /* all of the above */
  extern int *string_length*(**void**);   /* the length of the string */

I use a character array called *string_mem* to store these strings. Strings in the *string_mem* are never deallocated, so memory management is simple. When the scanner has identified a string, it will add it to the current string using *add_string*. The scanner can then decide when to start a new string by calling *new_string* and when the string is ready for permanent storage by calling *end_string*. *string_length* returns the length of the current string.

Some statistics: `tex.web` contains 11195 Strings with an average of 46.6 characters per string and a maximum of 5234 characters (the text in limbo); the second largest string has 1891 characters. The total number of characters in all strings is 516646. (Scanning `etex.web` will require even more string memory.)

⟨ internal declarations 3 ⟩ +≡ (28)
#define MAX_STRING_MEM 800000

⟨ global variables 11 ⟩ +≡ (29)
  static char $string\_mem\,[\texttt{MAX\_STRING\_MEM}]$;
  static int $free\_strings = \texttt{MAX\_STRING\_MEM}$;
  static int $current\_string = 0$;

⟨ show summary 12 ⟩ +≡ (30)
  DBG($dbgbasic$, "free_strings_=_%d\n", $free\_strings$);

The string currently under construction is identified by the position of its first character, the $current\_string$, and its last character MAX_STRING_MEM $-\,free\_strings$.

⟨ functions 13 ⟩ +≡ (31)
  char $*new\_string\,(\textbf{void})$
  {
    $current\_string = \texttt{MAX\_STRING\_MEM} - free\_strings$;
    return $string\_mem + current\_string$;
  }
  void $add\_string\,(\textbf{char} *str)$
  {
    while ($free\_strings > 0$) {
      if ($*str \ne 0$) $string\_mem\,[\texttt{MAX\_STRING\_MEM} - free\_strings\,\text{--}\,] = *str\text{++}$;
      else return;
    }
    ERROR("String_mem_overflow");
  }
  char $*end\_string\,(\textbf{void})$
  {
    char $*str = string\_mem + current\_string$;
    if ($free\_strings > 0$) $string\_mem\,[\texttt{MAX\_STRING\_MEM} - free\_strings\,\text{--}\,] = 0$;
    else ERROR("String_mem_overflow");
    $current\_string = \texttt{MAX\_STRING\_MEM} - free\_strings$; **return** str;
  }
  char $*copy\_string\,(\textbf{char} *str)$
  { $new\_string\,()$; $add\_string\,(str)$; **return** $end\_string\,()$; }
  int $string\_length\,(\textbf{void})$
  { **return** $(\texttt{MAX\_STRING\_MEM} - free\_strings) - current\_string$; }

3.5 Identifiers

To be able to parse the embedded Pascal code, I need to take special care of identifiers. I keep information related to identifiers in a table, called the *symbol_table*. The table is accessed by the string representing the identifier as a key and it returns a pointer to the table entry, called a **symbol**.

⟨ external declarations 5 ⟩ +≡   (32)
  typedef struct symbol {
    char *name*;
    int *tag*;
    int *obsolete*;
    int *for_ctrl*;
    int *value*;
    struct symbol *link*;
    token *type*;
    token *eq*;
  } **symbol**;
  extern int *get_sym_no*(**char** *name*);
  extern symbol *symbol_table*[ ];

⟨ internal declarations 3 ⟩ +≡   (33)
#**define** MAX_SYMBOL_TABLE   6007   /* or 4001 4999, a prime */
#**define** MAX_SYMBOLS   5200   /* must be less than MAX_SYMBOL_TABLE */

⟨ global variables 11 ⟩ +≡   (34)
  symbol *symbol_table*[MAX_SYMBOL_TABLE] = {NULL};
  static symbol *symbols*[MAX_SYMBOLS] = {{0}};
  static int *free_symbols* = MAX_SYMBOLS;

⟨ show summary 12 ⟩ +≡   (35)
  DBG(*dbgbasic*, "free␣symbols␣=␣%d\n", *free_symbols*);

I organize the symbol table as a hash table using double hashing as described in [7], Chapter 6.4.

⟨ functions 13 ⟩ +≡   (36)
  static int *symbol_hash*(**char** *name*)
  {
    int *hash* = 0;
    while (*name* ≠ 0) *hash* = *hash* + (*(*name*++) ⊕ #9E);
    return *hash*;
  }
  static symbol *new_symbol*(**void**)
  {
    CHECK(*free_symbols* > 0, "Symbol␣table␣overflow"); *free_symbols*−−;
    return *symbols* + *free_symbols*;
  }
  int *get_sym_no*(**char** *name*)
  {

```
    int i, c;
    i = symbol_hash(name) % MAX_SYMBOL_TABLE;
    if (symbol_table[i] ≠ NULL) {
      if (strcmp(symbol_table[i]→name, name) ≡ 0) return i;
      if (i ≡ 0) c = 1;
      else c = MAX_SYMBOL_TABLE − i;
      while (true) {
        i = i − c;
        if (i < 0) i = i + MAX_SYMBOL_TABLE;
        if (symbol_table[i] ≡ NULL) break;
        if (strcmp(symbol_table[i]→name, name) ≡ 0) return i;
      }
    }
    symbol_table[i] = new_symbol( ); symbol_table[i]→name = new_string( );
    add_string(name); end_string( ); symbol_table[i]→tag = ID; return i;
  }
```

The pointer into the symbol table can be stored inside the token in two ways: as an index into the *symbol_table* or as a direct pointer to the **symbol** structure. While scanning the WEB, I will assign the symbol number(*sym_no*), and while parsing Pascal, I will replace the symbol number by the symbol pointer (*sym_ptr*). This is necessary, because I will need to distinguish between various local symbols with the same name; these have only a single entry in the symbol table but the pointers will point to different **symbol** structures.

⟨ token specific info 8 ⟩ +≡ (37)
  int *sym_no*;
  struct symbol *sym_ptr*;

This leads to the following macros:

⟨ external declarations 5 ⟩ +≡ (38)
#**define** SYM_PTR(*name*) *symbol_table*[*get_sym_no*(*name*)]
#**define** SYMBOL
  { **int** *s* = *get_sym_no*(*yytext*); *add_token*(*symbol_table*[*s*]→*tag*)→*sym_no* = *s*; }
#**define** SYM(*t*) (*symbol_table*[(*t*)→*sym_no*])

It's easy to convert such a token back to a string.

⟨ convert token *t* to a string 39 ⟩ ≡ (39)
case ID: **case** PID: **case** PCONSTID: **case** PARRAYFILETYPEID:
  case PARRAYFILEID: **case** PFUNCID: **case** PPROCID: **case** PDEFVARID:
  case PDEFPARAMID: **case** PDEFREFID: **case** PDEFCONSTID:
  case PDEFTYPEID: **case** PDEFTYPESUBID: **case** PDEFFUNCID: **case** CREFID:
  case NMACRO: **case** OMACRO: **case** PMACRO:
  return SYM(*t*)→*name*;   Used in 99.

In TEX, like in most programs, I encounter two kinds of symbols: global and local symbols. While scanning, every symbol that I encounter gets entered into the global symbol table. While parsing, I will discover, that the variable *f* is a file variable in one function and an integer variable in another function. The two

3.5 Identifiers

occurrences of f have different scope. So I want to link different occurrences of f to different entries in the symbol table.

I use the function *localize* to create a local version of a symbol.

⟨external declarations 5⟩ +≡   (40)
  extern void *localize*(**token** *∗t*);

To open a new scope, I use the function *scope_open*; to close it again, I use the function *scope_close*.

⟨external declarations 5⟩ +≡   (41)
  extern void *scope_open*(**void**);
  extern void *scope_close*(**void**);

These functions use a small array holding all the symbol numbers of currently local symbols and another array to hold pointers to the global symbols of the same name.

⟨global variables 11⟩ +≡   (42)
#define MAX_LOCALS 50
  static int *locals*[MAX_LOCALS];
  static symbol *∗globals*[MAX_LOCALS];
  static int *free_locals* = MAX_LOCALS;

⟨functions 13⟩ +≡   (43)
  void *scope_open*(**void**)
  {
    CHECK(*free_locals* ≡ MAX_LOCALS,
      "Opening␣a␣new␣scope␣without␣closing␣the␣previous␣one");
  }
  void *scope_close*(**void**)
  {
    int *i*;
    for (*i* = *free_locals*; *i* < MAX_LOCALS; *i*++) *symbol_table*[*locals*[*i*]] = *globals*[*i*];
    free_locals = MAX_LOCALS;
  }

To localize a symbol, I create a new one and enter it, after saving the global symbol, into the symbol table.

⟨functions 13⟩ +≡   (44)
  void *localize*(**token** *∗t*)
  {
    int *sym_no* = *t*→*sym_no*;
    symbol *∗l, ∗g*;
    l = *new_symbol*( ); *g* = *symbol_table*[*sym_no*]; *l*→*name* = *g*→*name*;
    l→*tag* = *g*→*tag*; *l*→*eq* = *g*→*eq*; *symbol_table*[*sym_no*] = *l*;
    CHECK(*free_locals* > 0, "Overflow␣of␣local␣symbols␣in␣line␣%d",
      t→*lineno*); *free_locals* −−; *locals*[*free_locals*] = *sym_no*;
    globals[*free_locals*] = *g*; *t*→*sym_ptr* = *l*;
  }

3.6 Linking related tokens

So far I have considered the WEB file as one long flat list of tokens. As already mentioned above, the file has, however, also a nested structure: For example, each "{" token is related to a "}" token that ends either a TeX group or a Pascal comment. While scanning, I will need to know about this structure because it is necessary to do a correct switching of modes. Hence, I use the *link* field to connect the first token to the later token. This information is also useful at later stages, for example when I expand macros. The following table gives a list of related tokens.

Left	Right	Mode	Comment
(	)	PASCAL/PASCAL	needed for macro expansion
{	}	PASCAL/TEX/PASCAL	comments
{	}	MIDDLE/TEX/MIDDLE	comments
{	}	TEX/TEX	grouping
|	|	TEX/PASCAL/TEX	typesetting code
@<	@>		module names
=			begin of Pascal
==			begin of Pascal
	@	PASCAL	end of Pascal
	@*	PASCAL	end of Pascal
	@d	PASCAL	end of Pascal
	@f	PASCAL	end of Pascal
	@p	PASCAL	end of Pascal
"	"		list of WEB strings
@>=	@>=		continuation of module
@p	@p		continuation of program

Tab. 1: List of linked tokens

To track the nesting of structures, I need a stack:

⟨ global variables 11 ⟩ +≡ (45)
#**define** MAX_WWSTACK 200
 static token *$*wwstack$[MAX_WWSTACK] = \{0\}$;
 static int $wwsp = 0$;

I define the functions *ww_push* and *ww_pop* to operate on the stack. When popping a token, I keep the nesting information by linking it to its matching token. The function *ww_is* can be used to test the *tag* of the token on top of the stack.

⟨ external declarations 5 ⟩ +≡ (46)
 extern void *ww_push*(**token** *$*t$);
 extern token *$*ww\_pop$(**token** *$*t$);
 extern int *ww_is*(**int** *tag*);

3.6 Linking related tokens

⟨ functions 13 ⟩ +≡   (47)
  void ww_push(**token** $*left$)
  {
    CHECK($wwsp <$ MAX_WWSTACK, "WW␣stack␣overflow");
    DBG($dbglink$, "Pushing[%d]:", $wwsp$);
    if ($left \neq$ NULL) DBG($dbglink$, THE_TOKEN($left$));
    $wwstack[wwsp\mathord{+}\mathord{+}] = left$;
  }
  token $*ww\_pop$(**token** $*right$)
  {
    token $*left$;
    CHECK($wwsp > 0$, "Mode␣stack␣underflow"); $left = wwstack[\mathord{-}\mathord{-}wwsp]$;
    if ($left \neq$ NULL) $left \rightarrow link = right$;
    DBG($dbglink$, "Popping[%d]:", $wwsp$);
    if ($left \neq$ NULL) DBG($dbglink$, THE_TOKEN($left$));
    return $left$;
  }
  int ww_is(**int** tag)
  {
    return $wwsp > 0 \wedge wwstack[wwsp-1] \neq$ NULL $\wedge wwstack[wwsp-1] \rightarrow tag \equiv tag$;
  }

Using the stack, I can now also distinguish the use of "{" and "}" as a grouping construct in TEX from the use of starting and ending comments in Pascal. When I encounter "{" in TEX mode, it introduces a new level of grouping and I do not create a new token. Instead I push NULL on the stack. When I encounter "{" in PASCAL mode, however, it is the start of a comment; I create a token and push it. When I encounter the matching "}", I am always in TEX mode. I pop the stack and test the value: If it was NULL, I can continue in TEX mode because it was a grouping character; if it was not NULL, it is the end of a comment. I create a token for it and continue in PASCAL mode.

⟨ external declarations 5 ⟩ +≡   (48)
#define PUSH $ww\_push(last\_token)$
#define PUSH_NULL $ww\_push($NULL$)$
#define POP $ww\_pop(last\_token)$
#define POP_NULL   (ADD, POP)
#define POP_MLEFT   (EOS, TOK("}", RIGHT), BEGIN(MIDDLE), POP)
#define POP_PLEFT   (EOS, TOK("}", RIGHT), BEGIN(PASCAL), POP)
#define POP_LEFT
  (ww_is(MLEFT) ? POP_MLEFT : (ww_is(PLEFT) ? POP_PLEFT : POP_NULL))

Besides linking matching tokens, the *link* field can also be used to build linear list of related token. One example for such a list is the list of WEB strings. The program `tangle`, converting a WEB to Pascal, creates a string pool file. This mechanism is no longer available in `ctangle` so I have to implement an alternative (see section 5.8 on replacing the TEX string pool). Here I take the first step and collect all the strings that occur in the WEB in one linked list. For this purpose, I use a pointer to the *first_string*, and a pointer to the link field of the *last_string*. The macro WWSTRING is used in the scanner and adds the new string token to this list.

⟨external declarations 5⟩ +≡ (49)
  extern void *wwstring*(**char** **wwtext*);
#define WWSTRING   *wwstring*(*wwtext*)

⟨functions 13⟩ +≡ (50)
  void *wwstring*(**char** **wwtext*)
  {
    token **t* = *add_token*(STRING);
    t→sym_no = *get_sym_no*(*wwtext*); *t→text* = SYM(*t*)*→name*;
    *last_string = *t*; *last_string* = &(*t→link*);
  }

To make this work, it is sufficient to initialize the two pointers appropriately.

⟨global variables 11⟩ +≡ (51)
  static token **first_string* = NULL, ***last_string* = &*first_string*;

3.7 Module names

I need to maintain information for each module. I keep this information in a table, called the module table. The table is accessed by the string representing the module name as a key. This sounds very similar to what I did for identifiers, there is, however, one main difference: Modules are sometimes referenced by incomplete module names that end with an ellipsis (...). These incomplete module names may not even be valid TeX code. For this reason, I use a binary search tree to map module names to modules. The first thing I need, therefore, is a function to compare two module names. The function *module_cmp*(n, m) will compare the name of n to the name of m; it returns a negative value if $n < m$; zero if $n = m$; and a positive value if $n > m$. m is always a full module name, n might end abruptly with an ellipsis.

⟨functions 13⟩ +≡ (52)
  static int *module_name_cmp*(**token** **n*, **token** **m*)
  {
    n = *n→next*; *m* = *m→next*;   /* advance from "@<" to the name */
    if (*n→next→tag* ≡ ELIPSIS)
      return *strncmp*(*n→text*, *m→text*, *strlen*(*n→text*));
    else return *strcmp*(*n→text*, *m→text*);
  }

I organize the module table as a binary tree and allocate new modules from a large array.

⟨internal declarations 3⟩ +≡ (53)
#define MAX_MODULE_TABLE   1009   /* or 1009, 1231, 2017, 3001, a prime */

⟨global variables 11⟩ +≡ (54)
  static *module module_table*[MAX_MODULE_TABLE] = {{0}};

3.7 Module names

```
  static int free_modules = MAX_MODULE_TABLE;
  static module *module_root = NULL;
```

⟨ external declarations 5 ⟩ +≡ (55)
```
  typedef struct module {
    token *atless;
    token *atgreater;
    struct module *left, *right;
  } module;
  extern void add_module(token *atless);
  extern module *find_module(token *atless);
```

⟨ show summary 12 ⟩ +≡ (56)
```
  DBG(dbgbasic,"free␣modules␣=␣%d\n",free_modules);
```

To look up a module in the module table I use the function *find_module*. It returns a pointer to the module given the pointer to the "@<" token that starts the module name. The function will allocate a new module if needed.

⟨ functions 13 ⟩ +≡ (57)
```
  module *find_module(token *atless)
  {
    module **m = &module_root;
    while (*m ≠ NULL) {
      int d = module_name_cmp(atless,(*m)→atless);
      if (d ≡ 0) return *m;
      else if (d < 0) m = &((*m)→left);
      else m = &((*m)→right);
    }
    CHECK(free_modules > 0,"Module␣table␣overflow");
    *m = module_table + MAX_MODULE_TABLE − free_modules −−;
    (*m)→atless = atless; return *m;
  }
```

Because modules can be defined in multiple installments, I link together the closing "@>" tokens. This is done by calling the function *add_module* whenever I find the two tokens "@>=".

⟨ functions 13 ⟩ +≡ (58)
```
  void add_module(token *atless)
  {
    module *m = find_module(atless);
    token *atgreater = m→atgreater;
    if (atgreater ≡ NULL) m→atgreater = atless→link;
    else {
      while (atgreater→link ≠ NULL) atgreater = atgreater→link;
      atgreater→link = atless→link;
    }
  }
```

Next I consider the problem of scanning module names. The name of a module starts after a "@<" token. If this token shows up, I have to do some preparations depending on the current mode: If I am in TEX mode, I need to terminate the current TEXT token; if I am in MIDDLE mode, I pop the stack and terminate the macro or format definition I were just scanning; no special preparation is needed if I am in PASCAL mode. Then I push the "@<" token on the stack, start a new TEXT token, and switch to NAME mode. When I encounter the matching "@>" or "@>=" token, I add the module to the module table—calling *find_module* to cover the case that this is the first and only complete occurrence of the module name.

⟨external declarations 5⟩ +≡ (59)
#define AT_GREATER_EQ
    TOK("@>", ATGREATER), *add_module*(POP), TOK("=", EQ), PUSH, SEQ
#define AT_GREATER   TOK("@>", ATGREATER), *find_module*(POP)

You may have noticed that the above AT_GREATER_EQ macro pushes the EQ token on the stack. I match this token up with the token that ends the Pascal code following the equal sign. As you will see below, I do the same for macro definitions. Further, I link all the unnamed modules together using the "@p" tokens. I add an extra EQ token to match the convention that I have established for named modules.

⟨external declarations 5⟩ +≡ (60)
  extern token *∗program*;
#define PROGRAM
    (*program*→*link* = *last_token*, *program* = *last_token*), TOK("", EQ)

I use the first token as list head.

⟨global variables 11⟩ +≡ (61)
  token *∗program*;

⟨initialize token list 22⟩ +≡ (62)
  program = *first_token*;

3.8 Definitions

In a WEB file, the token "@d" introduces the definition of a numeric constants or a macro with or without parameter. When the scanner encounters such a token, it enters the DEFINITION mode.

The first token in DEFINITION mode is an identifier which will be stored in the symbol table. Then follows an optional macro parameter "(#)"; after the single or double equal sign, the scanner switches to MIDDLE mode, not without pushing the equal sign on the stack to be matched against the first token after the following Pascal code.

After scanning an "=" token, I know that a numeric macro is following, and I record this fact by changing the *tag* of the identifier in the token and in the symbol table.

⟨external declarations 5⟩ +≡ (63)
#define CHGTAG(t, x) $((t)\rightarrow tag = (x))$
#define CHGID(t, x) $(\text{SYM}(t)\rightarrow tag = (x))$
#define CHGTYPE(t, x) $(\text{SYM}(t)\rightarrow type = (x))$

3.9 Finishing the token list

#**define** CHGVALUE(t,x) (SYM$(t){\to}value = (x)$)
#**define** CHGTEXT(t,x) ($(t){\to}text = (x)$)

After scanning an "==" token, I know that I have either an ordinary macro or a parametrized macro. A PARAM token tells the difference.

⟨ functions 13 ⟩ +≡ (64)
  void *def_macro*(**token** *∗eq*, **int** *tag*)
  {
    token *∗id*;
    if ($eq{\to}previous{\to}tag \equiv$ PARAM) {
      $id = eq{\to}previous{\to}previous$; $tag =$ PMACRO;
    }
    else {
      $id = eq{\to}previous$;
    }
    CHGTAG(*id*, *tag*); CHGID(*id*, *tag*); SYM(*id*)$\to eq = eq$;
    DBG(*dbgexpand*, "Defining %s: %s\n", *tagname*(*tag*), SYM(*id*)$\to name$);
  }

⟨ external declarations 5 ⟩ +≡ (65)
  extern void *def_macro*(**token** *∗eq*, **int** *tag*);
#**define** DEF_MACRO(*tag*) *def_macro*(*last_token*, *tag*), SEQ

Similar, the token "@f" introduces a format specification switching the scanner to FORMAT mode. It then scans tokens until the first newline character brings the scanner back to MIDDLE mode.

3.9 Finishing the token list

When the scanner is done, I terminate the token list with two end of file tokens: one for Pascal and one for the WEB.

⟨ finalize token list 66 ⟩ ≡ (66)
  TOK("", ATP); PROGRAM; PUSH; TOK("", PEOF); TOK("", WEBEOF); POP Used in 4.

At this point I might want to have a complete list of all tokens and identifiers for debugging purposes.

⟨ finalize token list 66 ⟩ +≡ (67)
  if (*debugflags* & *dbgtoken*) {
    token $*t = \mathit{first\_token}$;
    while ($t \neq$ NULL) { MESSAGE(THE_TOKEN(t)); $t = t{\to}next$; }
  }
  if (*debugflags* & *dbgid*) {
    int *i*;
    for ($i = \mathit{free\_symbols}$; $i <$ MAX_SYMBOLS; $i{+}{+}$)
      MESSAGE("symbol[%d]=%s\n", *i*, *symbols*[*i*].*name*);
  }

4 Parsing Pascal

I use bison (the free replacement of yacc) to implement the parser. Fortunately TEX does not use the full Pascal language, so the parser can be simpler. Further, I do not need to generate code, but just analyze the Pascal programs for the purpose of finding those constructions where Pascal differs from C and need a conversion. If I discover such an instance, I change the tags of the affected tokens, set the *link* field to connect related tokens, or even construct a parse tree and link to it using the *up* field. In a next sweep over the token list in section 5, these changed tokens will help us make the appropriate transformations. But before I can do this, I need to feed the parser with the proper tokens, but not in the order I find them in the WEB file. I have to "tangle" them to get them into Pascal program order. The function that is supposed to deliver the tangled tokens is called *pplex*. In addition, the parser expects a function *pperror* to produce error messages.

⟨ external declarations 5 ⟩ +≡ (68)
   extern int *pplex*(**void**);
   extern void *pperror*(**const char** **message*);

The function *pperror* is very simple:

⟨ functions 13 ⟩ +≡ (69)
   void *pperror*(**const char** **message*)
   {
     ERROR("Parse␣error␣line␣%d:␣%s", *pplval*→*lineno*, *message*); }

4.1 Generating the sequence of Pascal tokens

Primarily, the Pascal tokens come from the unnamed modules and then from expanding module names and macros. Because modules and macros may reference other modules and macros, I will need a stack to keep track of where to continue expansion when I have reached the end of the current expansion.

⟨ global variables 11 ⟩ +≡ (70)
   #**define** MAX_PPSTACK   40
   static struct {
     token **next*, **end*, **link*;
     int *environment*;
     token **parameter*;
   } *pp_stack*[MAX_PPSTACK];
   static int *pp_sp* = MAX_PPSTACK;

In each stack entry, the pointers *next* and *end* point to the next and past the last token of the current replacement text. In the case of modules, where the replacement text for the module name might be defined in multiple installments, the *link* pointer is used to point to the continuation of the current replacement text.

In the *parameter* field, I store the pointer to the "(" token preceding the parameter of a parametrized macro; it provides us conveniently with a pointer to the parameter text with its *next* pointer and with its *link* pointer to the ")" token a pointer directly to the *end* of the parameter text. When I expand the parameter text of a parametrized macro, I need the *environment* variable. It points down the stack to the stack entry that contains the macro call. This is the place where I will find the replacement for a "#" token that might occur in the parameter text of nested parametrized macros.

The function *pp_push* will store the required information on the stack. Instead of passing the *next* and *end* pointer separately, I pass a pointer to the "=" token from the macro or module definition. This token conveniently contains both pointers. The function then advances the stack pointer, initializes the new stack entry, and returns the pointer to the first token of the replacement. *pp_pop* will pop the stack and again return the pointer to the next token.

⟨ functions 13 ⟩ +≡ (71)
  token *pp_push(**token** *$link$, **token** *eq, **int** $environment$, **token** *$parameter$)
  {
    CHECK($pp\_sp > 0$, "Pascal␣lexer␣stack␣overflow"); pp_sp --;
    $pp\_stack[pp\_sp].link = link$; $pp\_stack[pp\_sp].next = eq \rightarrow next$;
    $pp\_stack[pp\_sp].end = eq \rightarrow link$;
    $pp\_stack[pp\_sp].environment = environment$;
    $pp\_stack[pp\_sp].parameter = parameter$;
    DBG($dbgexpand$, "Push␣pplex[%d]:␣", MAX_PPSTACK $- pp\_sp$);
    DBGTOKS($dbgexpand$, $eq \rightarrow next$, $eq \rightarrow link$); **return** $pp\_stack[pp\_sp].next$;
  }
  token *pp_pop(**void**)
  {
    CHECK($pp\_sp <$ MAX_PPSTACK, "Pascal␣Lexer␣stack␣underflow");
    pp_sp ++; DBG($dbgexpand$, "Pop␣pplex[%d]:␣", MAX_PPSTACK $- pp\_sp$);
    DBGTOKS($dbgexpand$, $pp\_stack[pp\_sp].next$, $pp\_stack[pp\_sp].end$);
    return $pp\_stack[pp\_sp].next$;
  }

The function *pplex* is what I write next. In an "endless" loop, I read the next token from the stack just described, popping and pushing the stack as necessary. If I find a Pascal token—it has a *tag* value greater than FIRST_PASCAL_TOKEN—I can return its *tag* immediately to the parser. WEB tokens receive special treatment. When I deliver a token to the parser, *pplval*, the semantic value of the token, is the token pointer itself.

⟨ functions 13 ⟩ +≡ (72)
  int $pplex$(**void**)

4.2 Simple cases for the parser

```
{
  token *t;
  int tag;
  t = pp_stack[pp_sp].next;
  while (true) {
    if (t ≡ pp_stack[pp_sp].end) {
      ⟨process the end of a code segment 87⟩
      continue;
    }
    tag = t→tag;
  tag_known:
    if (tag > FIRST_PASCAL_TOKEN) {
      pp_stack[pp_sp].next = t→next; goto found;
    }
    else {
      switch (tag) {
        ⟨special treatment for WEB tokens 73⟩
        default: ERROR("Unexpected␣token␣in␣pplex:"THE_TOKEN(t));
      }
    }
  }
 found:
  DBG(dbgpascal, "pplex:␣%s->\t", tagname(tag));
  DBG(dbgpascal, THE_TOKEN(t));
  if (pascal ≠ NULL) fprintf(pascal, "%s␣", token2string(t));
  pplval = t; return tag;
}
```

4.2 Simple cases for the parser

Now let's look at all the WEB tokens and what *pplex* should to do with them. Quite a lot of them can be simply skipped:

⟨special treatment for WEB tokens 73⟩ ≡   (73)
case NL: **case** INDENT:
  if (*pascal* ≠ NULL) *fprintf* (*pascal*, "%s", *token2string* (*t*));
case METACOMMENT: **case** ATT: **case** ATEX: **case** ATQM: **case** ATPLUS:
  case ATSLASH: **case** ATBACKSLASH: **case** ATBAR: **case** ATHASH:
  case ATCOMMA: **case** ATINDEX: **case** ATINDEXTT: **case** ATINDEX9:
  case ATAND: **case** ATSEMICOLON: **case** ATLEFT: **case** ATRIGHT:
  $t = t \to next$; **continue**;   Used in 72.

Comments can be skipped in a single step:

⟨special treatment for WEB tokens 73⟩ +≡   (74)
case MLEFT: **case** PLEFT: $t = t \to link \to next$; **continue**;

The Pascal end-of-file token is passed to the parser which then should terminate.

⟨special treatment for WEB tokens 73⟩ +≡   (75)

case PEOF: $pp\_stack[pp\_sp].next = t{\to}next$; **goto** *found*;

Simple is also the translation of octal or hexadecimal constants and single character strings: I translate them as Pascal integers. The token "@$", it's the string pool checksum, is an integer as well.

⟨ special treatment for WEB tokens 73 ⟩ +≡ (76)
case ATDOLLAR: **case** OCTAL: **case** HEX: **case** CHAR:
  $pp\_stack[pp\_sp].next = t{\to}next$; $tag = $ PINTEGER; **goto** *found*;

The last simple case are identifiers. For identifiers, I find the correct tag in the symbol table which is maintained by the parser. At this point, I give tokens that still have the $tag \equiv $ ID the default tag PID and link tokens to the actual symbol structure, which might be local or global.

⟨ special treatment for WEB tokens 73 ⟩ +≡ (77)
case ID:
  {
    symbol $*s = $ SYM(t);
    $tag = s{\to}tag$;
    if $(tag \equiv $ ID$)$ $tag = s{\to}tag = $ PID;
    $t{\to}sym\_ptr = s$; $t{\to}tag = tag$; **goto** *tag_known*;
  }

4.3 The macros debug, gubed, and friends

TEX does some special trickery with the pseudo keywords **debug**, **gubed**, **init**, **tini**, **stat**, and **tats**. These identifiers are used to generate different versions of TEX for debugging, initialization, and gathering of statistics. The natural way to do this in C is the use of # **ifdef**...# **endif**. It is however not possible in C to define a macro like "# **define debug** # **ifdef** DEBUG" because the C preprocessor performs a simple one-pass replacement on the source code. So macros are expanded and the expansion is not expanded a second time.

It would be possible to define a module ⟨ debug 123 ⟩ that ctangle expands to "# **ifdef** DEBUG" before the C preprocessor sees it; the other possibility is to do the expansion right now in web2w. The latter possibility is simple, so I do it here, but it affects the visual appearance of the converted code to its disadvantage.

There are further possibilities too: I could redefine the macro as "# **define debug** **if** $(Debug)$ {" making it plain C code. Then the compiler would insert or optimize away the code in question depending on whether I say "# **define** *Debug* 1" or "# **define** *Debug* 0". The **stat**...**tats** brackets are however often used to enclose variable- or function-definitions where an "**if** $(Debug)$ {" would not work.

There are, however, also instances where the "# **ifdef** DEBUG" approach does not work. For instance, **debug**...**gubed** is used inside the macro *succumb*. Fortunately there are only a few of these instances and I deal with them in the patch file.

As far as the parser is concerned, I just skip these tokens.

⟨ special treatment for WEB tokens 73 ⟩ +≡ (78)

4.3 The macros debug, gubed, and friends

case WDEBUG: **case** WGUBED: **case** WINIT: **case** WTINI: **case** WSTAT:
  case WTATS: $t = t \rightarrow next$; **continue**;

Later, I get them back into the cweb file using the following code. It takes care not to replace the special keywords when they are enclosed between vertical bars and are only part of the descriptive text.

⟨convert t from WEB to cweb 79⟩ ≡ (79)
case WDEBUG:
  if $(t \rightarrow previous \rightarrow tag \equiv \text{BAR})$ $wputs(t \rightarrow text)$;
  else {
    if $(column \neq 0)$ $wput(\text{'}\backslash \text{n'})$;
    $wputs(\texttt{"\#ifdef\textvisiblespace @!DEBUG\textbackslash n"})$;
  }
  $t = t \rightarrow next$; **break**;
case WINIT:
  if $(t \rightarrow previous \rightarrow tag \equiv \text{BAR})$ $wputs(t \rightarrow text)$;
  else {
    if $(column \neq 0)$ $wput(\text{'}\backslash \text{n'})$;
    $wputs(\texttt{"\#ifdef\textvisiblespace @!INIT\textbackslash n"})$;
  }
  $t = t \rightarrow next$; **break**;
case WSTAT:
  if $(t \rightarrow previous \rightarrow tag \equiv \text{BAR})$ $wputs(t \rightarrow text)$;
  else {
    if $(column \neq 0)$ $wput(\text{'}\backslash \text{n'})$;
    $wputs(\texttt{"\#ifdef\textvisiblespace @!STAT\textbackslash n"})$;
  }
  $t = t \rightarrow next$; **break**;
case WGUBED: **case** WTINI: **case** WTATS:
  if $(t \rightarrow previous \rightarrow tag \equiv \text{BAR})$ $wputs(t \rightarrow text)$;
  else {
    if $(column \neq 0)$ $wput(\text{'}\backslash \text{n'})$;
    $wputs(\texttt{"\#endif\textbackslash n"})$;
  }
  $t = t \rightarrow next$;
  if $(t \rightarrow tag \equiv \text{ATPLUS} \lor t \rightarrow tag \equiv \text{ATSLASH})$ $t = t \rightarrow next$;
  if $(t \rightarrow tag \equiv \text{NL})$ $t = t \rightarrow next$;
  break;
                                                                Used in 101.

I ignore "@+" tokens that precede **debug** and friends, because their replacement should always start on the beginning of a line.

⟨convert t from WEB to cweb 79⟩ +≡ (80)
case ATPLUS: $t = t \rightarrow next$;
  if $(\neg following\_directive(t))$ $wputs(\texttt{"@+"})$;
  else DBG$(dbgcweb, \texttt{"Eliminating\textvisiblespace @+\textvisiblespace in\textvisiblespace line\textvisiblespace \%d\textbackslash n"}, t \rightarrow lineno)$; **break**;

Because they also occur in format definitions, I mark the identifiers as obsolete.

⟨ finalize token list 66 ⟩ +≡ (81)
   SYM_PTR("debug")→$obsolete = 1$; SYM_PTR("gubed")→$obsolete = 1$;
   SYM_PTR("stat")→$obsolete = 1$; SYM_PTR("tats")→$obsolete = 1$;
   SYM_PTR("init")→$obsolete = 1$; SYM_PTR("tini")→$obsolete = 1$;

4.4 Parsing numerical constants

I do not expand numerical macros, instead I expand the Pascal grammar to handle NMACRO tokens. This is also the right place to switch numeric macros from symbol numbers to symbol pointers. For each use of the token, I increment its *value* field in the symbol table. This will allow us later to eliminate definitions that are no longer used. The handling of WEB strings is similar.

⟨ special treatment for WEB tokens 73 ⟩ +≡ (82)
case NMACRO: $t{\to}sym_ptr = $ SYM(t);
  if $(t{\to}sym_ptr{\to}eq{\to}next{\to}tag \equiv $ STRING$)$ {
    token $*s = t{\to}sym\_ptr{\to}eq{\to}next$;
    $s{\to}sym_ptr = $ SYM(s); $s{\to}sym\_ptr{\to}value$++;
    DBG($dbgstring$, "Using numeric macro %s (%d) in line %d\n",
        $s{\to}sym\_ptr{\to}name, s{\to}sym\_ptr{\to}value, t{\to}lineno$);
  }
  $pp\_stack[pp\_sp].next = t{\to}next$; **goto** *found*;
case STRING: $t{\to}sym_ptr = $ SYM(t); $t{\to}sym\_ptr{\to}value$++;
  DBG($dbgstring$, "Using string %s (%d) in line %d\n", $t{\to}sym\_ptr{\to}name$,
    $t{\to}sym\_ptr{\to}value, t{\to}lineno$); $pp\_stack[pp\_sp].next = t{\to}next$;
goto *found*;

Occasionally, I will need the ability to determine the value of a token that the Pascal parser considers an integer. The function *getval* will return this value.

⟨ external declarations 5 ⟩ +≡ (83)
  extern int *getval*(**token** $*t$);

⟨ functions 13 ⟩ +≡ (84)
  int *getval*(**token** $*t$)
  {
    int $n = 0$;
    switch $(t{\to}tag)$ {
    case ATDOLLAR: $n = 0$; **break**;
    case PINTEGER: $n = strtol(t{\to}text, $ NULL$, 10)$; **break**;
    case NMACRO: $t = $ SYM$(t){\to}eq$; CHECK$(t{\to}tag \equiv $ EQEQ,
        "= expected in numeric macro in line %d", $t{\to}lineno$);
    $t = t{\to}next$;
    if $(t{\to}tag \equiv $ PMINUS$)$ {
      $t = t{\to}next$; $n = -getval(t)$;
    }
    else $n = getval(t)$;
    while $(true)$ {
      if $(t{\to}next{\to}tag \equiv $ PPLUS$)$ {

4.5 Expanding module names and macros

```
        t = t→next→next;  n = n + getval(t);
      }
      else if (t→next→tag ≡ PMINUS) {
        t = t→next→next;  n = n − getval(t);
      }
      else break;
    }
    break;
  case OCTAL:    n = strtol(t→text + 2, NULL, 8);  break;
  case HEX:      n = strtol(t→text + 2, NULL, 16);  break;
  case CHAR:     n = (int)(unsigned char) t→text[1];  break;
  case PCONSTID: n = SYM(t)→value;  break;
  default: ERROR("Unable␣to␣get␣value␣for␣tag␣%s␣in␣line␣%d", TAG(t),
      t→lineno);
  }
  return n;
}
```

Notice that I assume that tokens which are tagged as constant identifiers are expected to have a value stored in the symbol table. We write this value using the macro SETVAL.

⟨external declarations 5⟩ +≡   (85)
#**define** SETVAL(t, val) SYM(t)→$value = val$

4.5 Expanding module names and macros

Now let's turn to the more complicated operations, for example the expansion of module names. I know that I hit a module name when I encounter an "@<" token. At this point, I advance the current token pointer past the end of the module name, look up the module in the module table, and push its first code segment.

⟨special treatment for WEB tokens 73⟩ +≡   (86)
case ATLESS:
  {
    token ∗eq, ∗$atgreater$;
    $atgreater = $ find_module(t)→$atgreater$;
    CHECK($atgreater \neq$ NULL, "Undefined␣module␣@<%s␣...@>␣in␣line␣%d",
        token2string(t→$next$), t→$lineno$);
    DBG($dbgexpand$, "Expanding␣module␣@<%s@>␣in␣line␣%d\n",
        token2string(t→$next$), t→$lineno$); $eq = atgreater$→$next$;
    $pp\_stack[pp\_sp].next = t$→$link$→$next$;
    $t = $ pp_push($atgreater$→$link, eq, 0, $NULL); **continue**;
  }

When I reach the end of the code segment, I can check the link field to find its continuation.

⟨process the end of a code segment 87⟩ ≡   (87)
  token ∗$link = pp\_stack[pp\_sp].link$;

```
if (link ≠ NULL) {
    token *eq;
    eq = link→next;  link = link→link;  pp_pop( );
    t = pp_push(link, eq, 0, NULL);
}
else  t = pp_pop( );                                                           Used in 72.
```
Slightly simpler are ordinary macros.

⟨ special treatment for WEB tokens 73 ⟩ +≡   (88)
```
case OMACRO:
    {
      token *eq;
      eq = SYM(t)→eq;  pp_stack[pp_sp].next = t→next;
      DBG(dbgexpand, "Expanding␣ordinary␣macro␣%s␣in␣line␣%d\n",
            token2string(t), t→lineno);  t = pp_push(NULL, eq, 0, NULL);  continue;
    }
```

There are a few macros, that are special; I do not want to expand them but instead generate special tokens in web.1 and expand the Pascal grammar to cope with them directly. It remains, however, to mark them as obsolete to remove the macro definitions form the cweb output.

⟨ finalize token list 66 ⟩ +≡   (89)
```
    SYM_PTR("return")→obsolete = 1;  SYM_PTR("endcases")→obsolete = 1;
    SYM_PTR("othercases")→obsolete = 1;  SYM_PTR("mtype")→obsolete = 1;
    SYM_PTR("final_end")→obsolete = 1;
```

4.6 Expanding macros with parameters

Now I come to the most complex case: parametrized macros. When the WEB invokes a parametrized macro as part of the Pascal code, the macro identifier is followed by a "(" token, the parameter tokens, and a matching ")" token. The WEB scanner has also set the *link* field of the "(" token to point to the ")" token. The replacement text for the macro is found in the same way as for ordinary macros above. The replacement text, however, may now contain a "#" token, asking for another replacement by the parameter tokens. The whole process can be nested because the parameter tokens may again contain a "#" token. Hence, I need to store the parameter tokens on the stack as well as a reference to the enclosing environment. I store a reference to the "(" token on the stack, because from it, I can get the first token and the last token of the replacement text.

I can write now the code to expand a parametrized macro. To cope with cases like font(x), font == type and type(#)=mem[#], I call *pplex* to find the opening parenthesis before pushing the macro expansion and its parameter. (Note: I expand font as an ordinary macro; then find type which is a parametrized macro and end up in the "**case** PMACRO:" below. The "(" token is not the next token after type because I am still expanding font. Calling *pplex* will reach the end of the expansion, pop the stack, and then find the "(" token.)

⟨ special treatment for WEB tokens 73 ⟩ +≡   (90)

case PMACRO:
  {
    token *$open$, *eq;
    int $popen$;
    DBG($dbgexpand$, "Expanding␣parameter␣macro␣%s␣in␣line␣%d\n",
        $token2string(t), t{\rightarrow}lineno$); $eq = $ SYM$(t){\rightarrow}eq$;
    $pp\_stack[pp\_sp].next = t{\rightarrow}next$; $popen = pplex()$;
    CHECK($popen \equiv $ POPEN, "expected␣(␣after␣macro␣with␣parameter");
    $open = pplval$; $pp\_stack[pp\_sp].next = open{\rightarrow}link{\rightarrow}next$;
    ⟨count macro parameters 144⟩
    $t = pp\_push($NULL$, eq, pp\_sp, open)$; **continue**;
  }

While traversing the replacement text, I may find a "#" token. In this case, I find on the pp_stack the pointer to the *parameter* and, in case the *parameter* contains again a "#" token, its *environment*.

⟨special treatment for WEB tokens 73⟩ +≡   (91)
case HASH:
  {
    token *$parameter = pp\_stack[pp\_sp].parameter$;
    int $environment = pp\_stack[pp\_sp].environment$;
    $pp\_stack[pp\_sp].next = t{\rightarrow}next$; $t = pp\_push($NULL$, parameter,$
        $pp\_stack[environment].environment, pp\_stack[environment].parameter)$;
    continue;
  }

4.7 The function *ppparse*

The function *ppparse* is implemented in the file pascal.y which must be processed by bison (the free version of yacc) to produce pascal.tab.c and pascal.tab.h. The former contains the definition of the parser function *ppparse* which I call after initializing the *pp_stack* in preparation for the first call to *pplex*.

⟨parse Pascal 92⟩ ≡   (92)
  $program = first\_token{\rightarrow}link$; $pp_push(program{\rightarrow}link, program{\rightarrow}next, 0, $NULL$)$;
  $ppparse()$;   Used in 1.

The function *ppparse* occasionally builds a parse tree out of internal nodes for the Pascal program; this parse tree is then used to accomplish the transformations needed to turn the Pascal code into C code.

⟨internal node 93⟩ ≡   (93)
  struct {
    int $value$;
  }   Used in 6.

Internal nodes are constructed using the function *join*.

⟨external declarations 5⟩ +≡   (94)
  token *$join($**int** tag, **token** *$left$, **token** *$right$, **int** $value)$;

⟨ functions 13 ⟩ +≡ (95)
  token *$join$(**int** tag, **token** *$left$, **token** *$right$, **int** $value$)
  {
    token *$n = new\_token(tag)$;
    $n{\to}previous = left$; $n{\to}next = right$; $n{\to}value = value$;
    DBG($dbgjoin$, "tree: ");   DBGTREE($dbgjoin, n$);   **return** n;
  }

5 Writing the cweb

5.1 cweb output routines

The basic function to write the cweb file is the function *wprint*, along with its simpler cousins *wput* and *wputs*, and the more specialized member of the family *wputi*. While most of the work of converting the visual representation of tokens to cweb is left to the function *token2string*, the basic functions take care of inserting spaces after a comma and to prevent adjacent tokens from running together.

The variables *alfanum* and *comma* indicate that the last character written was alphanumeric or a comma; the variable *column* counts the characters on the current line.

⟨global variables 11⟩ +≡   (96)
  static int *alfanum* = 0;
  static int *comma* = 0;
  static int *column* = 0;

⟨functions 13⟩ +≡   (97)
  static void *wput*(**char** *c*)
  {
    fputc(*c*, *w*); *alfanum* = *isalnum*(*c*); *comma* = *c* ≡ ',';
    if (*c* ≡ '\n') *column* = 0; **else** *column*++;
  }
  static void *wputs*(**char** *∗str*)
  {
    while (*∗str* ≠ 0) *wput*(*∗str*++);
  }
  static void *wputi*(**int** *i*)
  {
    if (*alfanum* ∨ *comma*) *fputc*('␣', *w*), *column*++;
    column += *fprintf*(*w*, "%d", *i*); *alfanum* = *true*; *comma* = *false*;
  }
  static void *wprint*(**char** *∗str*)
  {
    if ((*alfanum* ∨ *comma*) ∧ *isalnum*(*str*[0])) *fputc*('␣', *w*);
    wputs(*str*);
  }

Most tokens have their string representation stored in the *info.text* field, so I sketch the function *token2string* here and describe the details of conversion later.

⟨ internal declarations 3 ⟩ +≡ (98)
  static char *∗token2string*(**token** *∗t*);

⟨ functions 13 ⟩ +≡ (99)
  static char *∗token2string*(**token** *∗t*)
  {
    CHECK(*t* ≠ NULL, "Unable␣to␣convert␣NULL␣token␣to␣a␣string");
    switch (*t*→*tag*) {
    default:
      if (*t*→*text* ≠ NULL) **return** *t*→*text*;
      else return "";
      ⟨ convert token *t* to a string 39 ⟩
    }
  }

5.2 Traversing the WEB

After these preparations, I am ready to traverse the list of tokens again; this time not in Pascal order but in the order given in the WEB file because I want the cweb file to be as close as possible to the original WEB file.

The main loop can be performed by the function *wprint_to*. It traverses the token list until a given *last_token* is found. Using this function I can generate the whole cweb file simply by starting with the *first_token* and terminating with the *last_token*.

⟨ generate cweb output 100 ⟩ ≡ (100)
  wprint_to(*first_token*, *last_token*);
                                                                                                  Used in 1.

The function *wprint_to* delegates all the work to *wtoken* which in turn uses *wprint* and *token2string* after converting the tokens from WEB to cweb as necessary. Besides writing out the token, *wtoken* also advances past the written token and returns a pointer to the token immediately following it. The function *wtoken* will be called recursively. For debugging purposes, it maintains a counter of its nesting *level*.

⟨ functions 13 ⟩ +≡ (101)
  static token *∗wtoken*(**token** *∗t*)
  {
    static int *level* = 0;
    level++; DBG(*dbgcweb*, "wtoken[%d]␣%s␣(%s)␣line␣%d\n", *level*, TAG(*t*),
        token2string(*t*), *t*→*lineno*);
    switch (*t*→*tag*) {
      ⟨ convert *t* from WEB to cweb 79 ⟩
    default: *wprint*(*token2string*(*t*)); *t* = *t*→*next*; **break**;
    }
    level−−; **return** *t*;
  }

5.3 Simple cases of conversion

wprint_to is complemented by the function *wskip_to* which suppresses the printing of tokens.

⟨internal declarations 3⟩ +≡ (102)
  static token *∗wprint_to*(**token** *∗t*, **token** *∗end*);
  static token *∗wskip_to*(**token** *∗t*, **token** *∗end*);

⟨functions 13⟩ +≡ (103)
  static token *∗wprint_to*(**token** *∗t*, **token** *∗end*)
  {
    while $(t \ne end)$ $t = wtoken(t)$;
    return t;
  }
  static token *∗wskip_to*(**token** *∗t*, **token** *∗end*)
  {
    while $(t \ne end)$ $t = t \rightarrow next$;
    return t;
  }

5.3 Simple cases of conversion

Quite a few tokens serve a syntactical purpose in Pascal but are simply ignored when generating C code.

⟨convert t from WEB to cweb 79⟩ +≡ (104)
case CIGNORE: **case** PPROGRAM: **case** PLABEL: **case** PCONST: **case** PVAR:
  case PPACKED: **case** POF: **case** ATQM: **case** ATBACKSLASH:
    $t = t \rightarrow next$; **break**;

The parser will change a *tag* to CIGNORE by using the IGN macro.

⟨external declarations 5⟩ +≡ (105)
#define IGN(t) $((t) \rightarrow tag =$ CIGNORE)

TEX uses the control sequence "@t\2@>" after "**forward;**". It needs to be removed together with the forward declaration, because it does confuse cweb.

⟨convert t from WEB to cweb 79⟩ +≡ (106)
case PFORWARD:
  if $(t \rightarrow next \rightarrow tag \equiv$ PSEMICOLON) $wput(\text{'};\text{'}), t = t \rightarrow next \rightarrow next$;
  else $wprint(\text{"forward"}), t = t \rightarrow next$;
  if $(t \rightarrow tag \equiv$ ATT) $t = t \rightarrow next$;
  break;

The meta-comments of WEB are translated to plain C comments if they are just a single line and to **#if 0**...**#endif** otherwise.

⟨convert t from WEB to cweb 79⟩ +≡ (107)
case METACOMMENT:
  {
    char *∗c*;
    $wputs(\text{"/*"})$;
    for $(c = t \rightarrow text + 2;\ c[0] \ne \text{'@'} \lor c[1] \ne \text{'}\}\text{'};\ c\texttt{++})\ wput(*c)$;

```
    wputs("*/"); t = t→next;
  }
  break;
case ATLEFT:
  if (column ≠ 0) wput('\n');
  wputs("#if␣0\n"); t = t→next; break;
case ATRIGHT:
  if (column ≠ 0) wput('\n');
  wputs("#endif\n"); t = t→next; break;
```

Some tokens just need a slight adjustment of their textual representation. In other cases, the parser changes the tag of a token, for example to PSEMICOLON, without changing the textual representation of that token. All these tokens are listed below.

⟨ convert t from WEB to cweb 79 ⟩ +≡   (108)
```
case PLEFT: case MLEFT: wputs("␣/*"); t = t→next; break;
case RIGHT: wputs("*/␣"); t = t→next; break;
case PSEMICOLON: wputs(";"); t = t→next; break;
case PCOMMA: wputs(","); t = t→next; break;
case PMOD: wput('%'); t = t→next; break;
case PDIV: wput('/'); t = t→next; break;
case PNIL: wprint("NULL"); t = t→next; break;
case POR: wputs("||"); t = t→next; break;
case PAND: wputs("&&"); t = t→next; break;
case PNOT: wputs("!"); t = t→next; break;
case PIF: wprint("if␣("); t = t→next; break;
case PTHEN: wputs(")␣"); t = t→next; break;
case PASSIGN: wput('='); t = t→next; break;
case PNOTEQ: wputs("!="); t = t→next; break;
case PEQ: wputs("=="); t = t→next; break;
case EQEQ: wput('\t'); t = t→next; break;
case OCTAL: wprint("0"); wputs(t→text + 2); t = t→next; break;
case HEX: wprint("0x"); wputs(t→text + 2); t = t→next; break;
case PTYPEINT: wprint("int"); t = t→next; break;
case PTYPEREAL: wprint("double"); t = t→next; break;
case PTYPEBOOL: wprint("bool"); t = t→next; break;
case PTYPECHAR: wprint("unsigned␣char"); t = t→next; break;
```

I convert "**begin**" to "{". In most cases, I want an "@+" to follow; except of course if a preprocessor directive is following.

⟨ convert t from WEB to cweb 79 ⟩ +≡   (109)
```
case PBEGIN: wput('{'), t = t→next;
  if (¬following_directive(t)) wputs("@+");
  break;
```

⟨ internal declarations 3 ⟩ +≡   (110)
  static bool *following_directive*(**token** *t);

5.4 Pascal division

⟨ functions 13 ⟩ +≡   (111)
  static bool *following_directive*(**token** *t)
  {
    while (*true*)
      if (WDEBUG ≤ t→tag ∧ t→tag ≤ WGUBED) **return** *true*;
      else if (t→tag ≡ ATPLUS ∨ t→tag ≡ ATEX ∨ t→tag ≡
          ATSEMICOLON ∨ t→tag ≡ NL ∨ t→tag ≡ INDENT) t = t→next;
      else return *false*;
  }

After the conversion, the Pascal token "$..$" will still occur in the file as part of code between vertical bars. To make it print nicely in the TEX output, it is converted to an identifier, "**dotdot**", that is used nowhere else.

⟨ convert t from WEB to cweb 79 ⟩ +≡   (112)
case PDOTDOT: *wprint*("dotdot"); t = t→next; **break**;

Using the patch file, I instruct cweave to treat this identifier in a special way and print it like "$..$".

5.4 Pascal division

In some cases build-in functions of Pascal can be replaced by a suitably defined macro in C. The most simple solution was to add these definitions to the module "⟨ Compiler directives ⟩" using the patch file. Using Macros instead of inline replacement has the advantage that the visual appearance of the original code remains undisturbed. A not so simple case is the Pascal division.

The Pascal language has two different division operators: "**div**" divides two integers and gives an integer result; it can be replaced by "/" in the C language. The Pascal operator "/" divides **integer** and **real** values and converts both operands to type **real** before doing so; replacing it simply by the C operator "/" will give different results if both operands are **integer** values because in this case C will do an integer division truncating the result. So expressions of the form "X/Y" should be replaced by "$X/$(**double**)(Y)" to force a floating point division in C

Fortunately, all expressions in the denominator have the form *total_stretch*[o], *total_shrink*[o], *glue_stretch*(r), *glue_shrink*(r), or *float_constant*(n). So no parentheses around the denominator are required and inserting a simple (**double**) after the / is sufficient. Further, the macro *float_constant* is already a cast to **double**, so I can check for the corresponding identifier and omit the extra cast.

⟨ global variables 11 ⟩ +≡   (113)
  static int *float_constant_no*;

⟨ initialize token list 22 ⟩ +≡   (114)
  float_constant_no = *predefine*("float_constant", ID, 0);

⟨ convert t from WEB to cweb 79 ⟩ +≡   (115)
case PSLASH: *wput*('/');
  if (t→next→tag ≠ PMACRO ∨ t→next→sym_no ≠ *float_constant_no*) {
    wprint("(double)");
    DBG(*dbgslash*, "Inserting␣(double)␣after␣/␣in␣line␣%d\n", t→*lineno*);

}
$t = t{\to}next;$ **break**;

5.5 Identifiers

Before I can look at the identifiers, I have to consider the "@!" token which can precede an identifier and will cause the identifiers to appear underlined in the index. The "@!" token needs a special treatment. When I convert Pascal to C, I have to rearrange the order of tokens and while I am doing so, a "@!" token that precedes an identifier should stick to the identifier and move with it. I accomplish this by suppressing the output of the "@!" token if it is followed by an identifier, and insert it again when I output the identifier itself.

⟨ convert t from WEB to cweb 79 ⟩ +≡   (116)
case ATEX: $t = t{\to}next;$
  if $(t{\to}tag \ne \text{ID} \wedge t{\to}tag \ne \text{PID} \wedge t{\to}tag \ne \text{PFUNCID} \wedge$
    $t{\to}tag \ne \text{PDEFVARID} \wedge t{\to}tag \ne \text{PDEFPARAMID} \wedge t{\to}tag \ne \text{PDEFTYPEID} \wedge$
    $t{\to}tag \ne \text{OMACRO} \wedge t{\to}tag \ne \text{PMACRO} \wedge t{\to}tag \ne \text{NMACRO} \wedge$
    $t{\to}tag \ne \text{CINTDEF} \wedge t{\to}tag \ne \text{CSTRDEF} \wedge t{\to}tag \ne \text{PDIV} \wedge$
    $t{\to}tag \ne \text{WDEBUG} \wedge t{\to}tag \ne \text{WINIT} \wedge t{\to}tag \ne \text{WSTAT})$ {
    $wputs(\texttt{"@!"});$ DBG$(dbgbasic, \texttt{"Tag\_after\_@!\_is\_\%s\_in\_line\_\%d\textbackslash n"},$
      $tagname(t{\to}tag), t{\to}lineno);$
  }
  break;

Identifier tokens are converted by using their name. I use a simple function to do the name lookup and take care of adding the "@!" token if necessary.

⟨ internal declarations 3 ⟩ +≡   (117)
  static void $wid(\textbf{token} *t);$

⟨ functions 13 ⟩ +≡   (118)
  void $wid(\textbf{token} *t)$
  {
    if $(alfanum \vee comma)$ $wput(\textrm{'\textvisiblespace'});$
    if $(t{\to}previous{\to}tag \equiv \text{ATEX})$ $wputs(\texttt{"@!"});$
    $wputs(\text{SYM}(t){\to}name);$
  }

I use this function like this:

⟨ convert t from WEB to cweb 79 ⟩ +≡   (119)
case ID: **case** PID: **case** OMACRO: **case** PMACRO: **case** NMACRO: $wid(t);$
  $t = t{\to}next;$ **break**;

Some identifiers that TEX uses are reserved words in C or loose their special meaning. So after I finish scanning the WEB, I change the names of these identifiers.

⟨ finalize token list 66 ⟩ +≡   (120)
  SYM_PTR($\texttt{"xclause"}$)${\to}name = \texttt{"else"};$
  SYM_PTR($\texttt{"switch"}$)${\to}name = \texttt{"get\_cur\_chr"};$
  SYM_PTR($\texttt{"continue"}$)${\to}name = \texttt{"resume"};$

```
SYM_PTR("exit")→name = "end"; SYM_PTR("free")→name = "is_free";
SYM_PTR("int")→name = "i"; SYM_PTR("remainder")→name = "rem";
```

A special case is the the field identifier **int**. It can not be used in C because it is a very common (if not the most common) reserved word. I replace it with i which does not conflict with the variable i because field names have their own name-space in C.

5.6 Strings

Pascal strings need some more work. I translate them to characters or C strings. Note that the parser occasionally converts STRING or CHAR tokens to PSTRING tokens.

⟨convert t from WEB to cweb 79⟩ +≡   (121)
case PCHAR:
 {
  char $*str = t{\to}text$;
  $wput(\textrm{'}\_\textrm{'})$; $wput(\textrm{'}\backslash\textrm{'}\textrm{'})$, $str{+}{+}$;
  if $(str[0] \equiv \textrm{'}\backslash\textrm{'}\textrm{'})$ $wputs(\texttt{"\textbackslash\textbackslash'"})$;
  else if $(str[0] \equiv \textrm{'}\backslash\backslash\textrm{'})$ $wputs(\texttt{"\textbackslash\textbackslash\textbackslash\textbackslash"})$;
  else if $(str[0] \equiv \textrm{'}@\textrm{'})$ $wputs(\texttt{"@@"})$;
  else $wput(str[0])$;
  $wput(\textrm{'}\backslash\textrm{'}\textrm{'})$; $wput(\textrm{'}\_\textrm{'})$;
 }
 $t = t{\to}next$; **break**;
case PSTRING:
 {
  char $*str = t{\to}text$;
  $wput(\textrm{'}\texttt{"}\textrm{'})$, $str{+}{+}$;
  while $(*str \neq 0)$ {
   if $(str[0] \equiv \textrm{'}\backslash\textrm{'}\textrm{'} \wedge str[1] \equiv \textrm{'}\backslash\textrm{'}\textrm{'})$ $wput(\textrm{'}\backslash\textrm{'}\textrm{'})$, $str{+}{+}$;
   else if $(str[0] \equiv \textrm{'}\texttt{"}\textrm{'} \wedge str[1] \equiv \textrm{'}\texttt{"}\textrm{'})$ $wputs(\texttt{"\textbackslash\textbackslash\textbackslash""})$, $str{+}{+}$;
   else if $(str[0] \equiv \textrm{'}\backslash\backslash\textrm{'})$ $wputs(\texttt{"\textbackslash\textbackslash\textbackslash\textbackslash"})$;
   else if $(str[0] \equiv \textrm{'}\backslash\textrm{'}\textrm{'} \wedge str[1] \equiv 0)$ $wput(\textrm{'}\texttt{"}\textrm{'})$;
   else if $(str[0] \equiv \textrm{'}\texttt{"}\textrm{'} \wedge str[1] \equiv 0)$ $wput(\textrm{'}\texttt{"}\textrm{'})$;
   else if $(str[0] \equiv \textrm{'}\texttt{"}\textrm{'})$ $wput(\textrm{'}\backslash\backslash\textrm{'})$, $wput(\textrm{'}\texttt{"}\textrm{'})$;
   else $wput(str[0])$;
   $str{+}{+}$;
  }
 }
 $t = t{\to}next$; **break**;

5.7 Module names

I have removed newlines and extra spaces from module names; now I have to insert newlines if the module names are too long.

⟨ convert t from WEB to cweb 79 ⟩ +≡   (122)
case ATLESS: $wputs($"@<"$); \ t = t \rightarrow next;$
  CHECK$(t \rightarrow tag \equiv$ TEXT, "Module␣name␣expected␣instead␣of␣%s␣in␣line␣%d",
    $token2string(t), t \rightarrow lineno);$
  {
    char $*str = t \rightarrow text;$
    do if $(str[0] \equiv$ '@' $\wedge str[1] \equiv$ ',') $str = str + 2;$
                                         /∗ control codes are forbidden in section names ∗/
    else if $(column > 80 \wedge isspace(*str)) \ wput($'\n'$), str ++;$
    else $wput(*str ++);$ **while** $(*str \neq 0);$
  }
  $t = t \rightarrow next;$
  if $(t \rightarrow tag \equiv$ ELIPSIS) $wputs($"..."$), t = t \rightarrow next;$
  CHECK$(t \rightarrow tag \equiv$ ATGREATER, "@>␣expected␣instead␣of␣%s␣in␣line␣%d",
    $token2string(t), t \rightarrow lineno); \ wputs($"@>"$); \ t = t \rightarrow next;$
  if $(t \rightarrow tag \equiv$ ATSLASH) $wputs($"@;"$), t = t \rightarrow next;$
  else if $(t \rightarrow tag \equiv$ PELSE $\vee (t \rightarrow tag \equiv$ NL)) $wputs($"@;"$);$
  break;

Note that I replace an "@/" after the module name by an "@;" Because in most places this is enough to cause the requested new line and causes the correct indentation.

5.8 Replacing the WEB string pool file

WEB strings need more work because I have to replace the WEB string pool file. Before I start, I finish two easy cases. Single character strings are replaced by C character constants. The string pool checksum is simply replaced by zero, because I will not use it.

⟨ convert t from WEB to cweb 79 ⟩ +≡   (123)
case CHAR:
  {
    char $c = t \rightarrow text[1];$
    $wput($'\''$);$
    if $(c \equiv$ '\'' $\vee c \equiv$ '\\') $wput($'\\'$);$
    $wput(c); \ wput($'\''$); \ t = t \rightarrow next;$ **break**;
  }
case ATDOLLAR: $wputs($"0"$); \ t = t \rightarrow next;$ **break**;

Of course it would be possible to generate suitable initializations for the variables *str_pool* and *str_start* and replace each string with its corresponding index in the *str_start* array. The goal of my project is, however, to generate readable source code and replacing for example "Maybe␣you␣should␣try␣asking␣a␣human?" by 283 is not very readable. Instead, I will create for each string a module, in the

5.8 Replacing the WEB string pool file

above example named ⟨"Maybe you should try asking a human?" 1234⟩, that will expand to the correct number, here 283.

⟨convert t from WEB to cweb 79⟩ +≡   (124)
case STRING:
  {
    ⟨convert some strings to macro names 125⟩
    else {
      $wputs$("@[@<|"); $wputs$(SYM(t)→$name$); $wputs$("|@>@]"); }
    $t = t$→$next$; **break**;
  }

There are some exceptions to the general rule, for example for the empty string. I define an appropriate constant *empty_string* and use it instead of a module (which would have a rather unsightly name). More instances of this scheme follow below.

⟨convert some strings to macro names 125⟩ ≡   (125)
  if (t→$sym\_no \equiv empty\_string\_no$) $wprint$("empty_string");   Used in 124.

To define all the other new modules, I add some code at the very end of the output file.

⟨generate cweb output 100⟩ +≡   (126)
  $wputs$("\n@␣Appendix:␣Replacement␣of␣the␣string␣pool␣file.\n");
  {
    token *str_k;
    int i, k;
    ⟨generate definitions for the first 256 strings 127⟩
    for ($str\_k = first\_string$; $str\_k \neq$ NULL; $str\_k = str\_k$→$link$)
      ⟨generate definition for string k 129⟩
    ⟨generate string pool initializations 140⟩
  }

The first 256 strings in the string pool are the printable replacements for the single character strings for all character codes from 0 to 255.

⟨generate definitions for the first 256 strings 127⟩ ≡   (127)
  $wputs$("@d␣str_0_255␣");
  for ($k = 0$; $k < 256$; k++) {
    if ((k & #F) ≡ 0) $wputs$("\t\"");
    if ((⟨Character k cannot be printed 128⟩)) {
      $wputs$("^^");
      if ($k < °100 \land k + °100 \equiv$ '@') $wputs$("@@");
      else if ($k < °100 \land k + °100 \equiv$ '\\') $wputs$("\\\\");
      else if ($k < °100$) $wput$($k + °100$);
      else if ($k < °200 \land k - °100 \equiv$ '@') $wputs$("@@");
      else if ($k < °200$) $wput$($k - °100$);
#**define** HEXDIGIT(x)   ((x) < 10 ? ((x) + '0') : ((x) − 10 + 'a'))
      else $wput$(HEXDIGIT($k/16$)), $wput$(HEXDIGIT($k \% 16$));
    }
    else if ($k \equiv$ '"') $wputs$("\\\"");

```
        else if (k ≡ '\\') wputs("\\\\");
        else if (k ≡ '@') wputs("@@");
        else wput(k);
        if ((k & #F) ≡ #F) wputs("\"@/\n");
      }
      wputs("@d␣str_start_0_255"); i = 0;
      for (k = 0; k < 256; k++) {
        if ((k & #F) ≡ 0) wput('\t');
        wputi(i);
        if ((⟨Character k cannot be printed 128⟩)) {
          if (k < °100) i = i + 3;
          else if (k < °200) i = i + 3;
          else i = i + 4;
        }
        else i = i + 1;
        wput(',');
        if ((k & #F) ≡ #F) wputs("@/\n");
      }
```
⟨ ⟩ Used in 126.

This condition is taken from tex.web:

⟨Character k cannot be printed 128⟩ ≡   (128)
$(k < \text{'}\sqcup\text{'}) \lor (k > \text{'}\sim\text{'})$

Used in 127.

⟨generate definition for string k 129⟩ ≡   (129)
```
      {
        symbol *s = SYM(str_k);
        if (s→value > 0) {
          s→value = 0; wputs("@␣\n");
          wputs("@d␣str_"), wputi(k), wput('␣'), wputs(s→name), wput('\n');
          ⟨generate macros for some strings 137⟩
          else wputs("@<|"), wputs(s→name), wputs("|@>=@+"), wputi(k);
          wput('\n'); k++;
        }
      }
```
Used in 126.

There are, however, a few more exceptions to the general procedure. Many of the WEB strings are used simply for printing with the procedure *print*. There is actually no need to enter all these strings into the string pool. Instead I add a procedure *print_str* that prints plain zero terminated C strings.

Now I can convert the STRING argument of the procedure *print* to a PSTRING by calling the following procedures in the parser.

⟨external declarations 5⟩ +≡   (130)
   extern void *pstring_args*(**token** **id*, **token** **arg*);
   extern void *pstring_assign*(**token** **id*, **token** **val*);

The function *pstring_args* is called with the *id* of the function. The *arg* token points to the argument list. A few other functions just pass their arguments to *print*. By replacing their call to *print* by a call to *print_str*, I can convert those

5.8 Replacing the WEB string pool file

arguments as well. For example the function *overflow* expects two arguments of which the first one is the STRING token. The other functions are: *prompt_file_name*, *print_nl*, and *fatal_error*.

If a STRING token is found, its *value* in the symbol table is decremented. This *value* counts the number of occurrences; if it goes down to zero, the STRING token is no longer used and no module needs to be generated for it.

⟨ functions 13 ⟩ +≡ (131)
```
  static int convert_arg(token *arg)
  {
    if (arg→tag ≡ STRING) {
      symbol *s = symbol_table[arg→sym_no];
      s→value −−;
      DBG(dbgstring, "Eliminating string argument %s (%d) in line %d\n",
          s→name, s→value, arg→lineno); arg→tag = PSTRING; return 1;
    }
    else if (arg→tag ≡ CHAR) {
      arg→tag = PSTRING; return 1;
    }
    return 0;
  }
  void pstring_args(token *id, token *arg)
  {
    if (arg→tag ≡ PCOLON ∨ arg→tag ≡ CREFID) return;
    if (id→sym_no ≡ overflow_no ∨ id→sym_no ≡ prompt_file_name_no) {
      CHECK(arg→tag ≡ PCOMMA,
            "function should have two arguments in line %d", id→lineno);
      convert_arg(arg→previous);
    }
    else if (id→sym_no ≡ print_no) {
      if (convert_arg(arg)) id→sym_no = print_str_no;
    }
    else if (id→sym_no ≡ print_str_no ∨ id→sym_no ≡ print_nl_no ∨ id→sym_no ≡
             fatal_error_no) convert_arg(arg);
  }
```

The function *pstring_assign* is used when STRING tokens are assigned to the variable *help_line*, which I redefine as a variable containing character pointers instead of string numbers.

⟨ functions 13 ⟩ +≡ (132)
```
  void pstring_assign(token *id, token *val)
  {
    if (id→tag ≡ PID ∧ (id→sym_no ≡ help_line_no ∨ id→sym_no ≡
        max_reg_help_line_no)) {
      SYM(val)→value −−; DBG(dbgstring,
          "Eliminating string assignment %s (%d) in line %d\n",
```

$\text{SYM}(val){\to}name, \text{SYM}(val){\to}value, val{\to}lineno);$
$val{\to}tag = \text{PSTRING};$
}
else DBG($dbgstring$, "No␣string␣assignment␣%s␣(%d)␣in␣line␣%d\n",
$\text{SYM}(val){\to}name, \text{SYM}(val){\to}value, val{\to}lineno);$
}

Note: $max\_reg\_help\_line$ is used in ϵ-TEX.

I have used these variables:

⟨ global variables 11 ⟩ +≡ (133)
    int $print\_no, print\_str\_no, overflow\_no, print\_err\_no, print\_nl\_no,$
        $fatal\_error\_no, prompt\_file\_name\_no, help\_line\_no, empty\_string\_no,$
        $max\_reg\_help\_line\_no;$

The variables are initialized like this:

⟨ functions 13 ⟩ +≡ (134)
    int $predefine$(**char** $*name$, **int** tag, **int** $value$)
    {
        int $sym\_no = get\_sym\_no(name);$
        symbol $*s = symbol\_table[sym\_no];$
        $s{\to}tag = tag; s{\to}value = value;$ **return** $sym\_no;$
    }

⟨ initialize token list 22 ⟩ +≡ (135)
    $print\_str\_no = predefine("print\_str", \text{PPROCID}, 0);$
    $empty\_string\_no = predefine("\backslash"\backslash"", \text{PID}, 1);$
    $help\_line\_no = predefine("help\_line", \text{ID}, 0);$
    $print\_no = predefine("print", \text{PPROCID}, 0);$
    $overflow\_no = predefine("overflow", \text{PPROCID}, 0);$
    $print\_err\_no = predefine("print\_err", \text{PPROCID}, 0);$
    $print\_nl\_no = predefine("print\_nl", \text{PPROCID}, 0);$
    $fatal\_error\_no = predefine("fatal\_error", \text{PPROCID}, 0);$
    $prompt\_file\_name\_no = predefine("prompt\_file\_name", \text{PPROCID}, 0);$
    $max\_reg\_help\_line\_no = predefine("max\_reg\_help\_line", \text{ID}, 0);$

There are still a few remaining problems. First, STRING tokens occur occasionally as part of a macro replacement text. There I can not substitute a module name for them. By having introduced the function $print\_str$, some of them are now plain C strings: "pool␣size" in line 1184 ($overflow$), "!␣" in line 1750 ($print\_nl$) "save␣size" in line 5910 ($overflow$), "input␣stack␣size" in line 6940 ($overflow$), "Font␣" in line 10927 ($print\_err$), "␣at␣" in line 10930 ($print$), "pt" in line 10930 ($print$), "␣scaled␣" in line 10933 ($print$), and "␣plus␣" in line 19250 ($print$).

Most other macros are numeric macros, and I just generate these instead of module names: "TeXinputs:" in line 9992 (TEX_area), "TeXfonts:" in line 9994 (TEX_font_area), ".fmt" in line 10082 ($format\_extension$), the $empty\_string$ in line 10928, and "0234000122*4000133**3**344*0400400*000000234000111*\
1111112341011" in line 15049 ($math\_spacing$).

5.8 Replacing the WEB string pool file

I have shown already some of the handling of the empty string; the rest follows now:

⟨ convert some strings to macro names 125 ⟩ +≡ (136)
    else if $(t\to sym\_no \equiv \textit{TeXinputs\_no})$ $wprint(\texttt{"TEX\_area"})$;
    else if $(t\to sym\_no \equiv \textit{TeXfonts\_no})$ $wprint(\texttt{"TEX\_font\_area"})$;
    else if $(t\to sym\_no \equiv \textit{fmt\_no})$ $wprint(\texttt{"format\_extension"})$;
    else if $(t\to sym\_no \equiv \textit{math\_spacing\_no})$ $wprint(\texttt{"math\_spacing"})$;

⟨ generate macros for some strings 137 ⟩ ≡ (137)
  if $(str\_k\to sym\_no \equiv \textit{empty\_string\_no})$ $wputs(\texttt{"@d␣empty\_string␣"}), wputi(k)$;
  else if $(str\_k\to sym\_no \equiv \textit{TeXinputs\_no})$ $wputs(\texttt{"@d␣TEX\_area␣"}), wputi(k)$;
  else if $(str\_k\to sym\_no \equiv \textit{TeXfonts\_no})$
    $wputs(\texttt{"@d␣TEX\_font\_area␣"}), wputi(k)$;
  else if $(str\_k\to sym\_no \equiv \textit{fmt\_no})$ $wputs(\texttt{"@d␣format\_extension␣"}), wputi(k)$;
  else if $(str\_k\to sym\_no \equiv \textit{math\_spacing\_no})$
    $wputs(\texttt{"@d␣math\_spacing␣"}), wputi(k)$;
                                                                                                   Used in 129.

⟨ global variables 11 ⟩ +≡ (138)
  int $\textit{TeXinputs\_no}, \textit{TeXfonts\_no}, \textit{fmt\_no}, \textit{math\_spacing\_no}$;

⟨ initialize token list 22 ⟩ +≡ (139)
  $\textit{TeXinputs\_no} = predefine(\texttt{"\textbackslash"TeXinputs:\textbackslash""}, \text{PID}, 0)$;
  $\textit{TeXfonts\_no} = predefine(\texttt{"\textbackslash"TeXfonts:\textbackslash""}, \text{PID}, 0)$;
  $\textit{fmt\_no} = predefine(\texttt{"\textbackslash".fmt\textbackslash""}, \text{PID}, 0)$;
  $\textit{math\_spacing\_no} = predefine(\texttt{"\textbackslash"0234000122*4000133**3**344*0400400*00\textbackslash}$
          $\texttt{0000234000111*1111112341011\textbackslash""}, \text{PID}, 1)$;

I am left with the macro *ensure_dvi_open*, containing `".dvi"` in line 10284, `"file␣name␣for␣output"` in line 10286, and `".dvi"` in line 10286, which I simply turn into a module of the same name using the patch file.

I conclude the generation of cweb output by generating initializations for the *str_pool* and *str_start* array.

⟨ generate string pool initializations 140 ⟩ ≡ (140)
  $wputs(\texttt{"\textbackslash n@␣All␣the␣above␣strings␣together␣make␣up␣the␣string␣pool.\textbackslash}$
      $\texttt{\textbackslash n" "@<|str\_pool|␣initialization@>=\textbackslash n" "str\_0\_255\textbackslash n"})$;
  for $(i = 256; i < k; i\mathrel{+}\mathrel{+})$ {
    $wputs(\texttt{"str\_"}), wputi(i)$;
    if $((i\mathbin{\&}7) \equiv 7)$ $wputs(\texttt{"@/\textbackslash n"})$; else $wput(\texttt{'␣'})$;
  }
  $wputs(\texttt{"\textbackslash n\textbackslash n@␣@<|str\_start|␣initialization@>=\textbackslash n" "str\_start\_0\_255\textbackslash n"})$;
  for $(i = 256; i < k; i\mathrel{+}\mathrel{+})$ {
    $wputs(\texttt{"str\_start\_"}), wputi(i), wput(\texttt{','})$;
    if $((i\mathbin{\&}3) \equiv 3)$ $wput(\texttt{'\textbackslash n'})$; else $wput(\texttt{'␣'})$;
  }
  $wputs(\texttt{"str\_start\_"}), wputi(k); wputs(\texttt{"\textbackslash n\textbackslash n"}$
    $\texttt{"@␣We␣still␣need␣to␣define␣the␣start␣locations␣of␣the␣strings.\textbackslash n"}$
    $\texttt{"@<prepare␣for␣string␣pool␣initialization@>=\textbackslash n"}$

```
"typedef␣enum␣{\n"
"str_start_256=sizeof(str_0_255)-1,\n");
```
for $(i = 257;\ i \leq k;\ i\texttt{++})$
$\quad wputs(\texttt{"str\_start\_"}), wputi(i), wputs(\texttt{"=str\_start\_"}), wputi(i-1),$
$\qquad wputs(\texttt{"+sizeof(str\_"}), wputi(i-1), wputs(\texttt{")-1,@/\textbackslash n"});$
$wputs(\texttt{"str\_start\_end␣}\}\texttt{␣str\_starts;\textbackslash n"}$
$\texttt{"\textbackslash n@␣@<|pool\_ptr|␣initialization@>=␣str\_start\_"}), wputi(k), wputs(\texttt{"\textbackslash n"}$
$\texttt{"\textbackslash n@␣@<|str\_ptr|␣initialization@>=␣"}), wputi(k), wput(\texttt{'\textbackslash n'}); \quad$ Used in 126.

5.9 Macro and format declarations

When I convert a macro, I first check if the translation has made it obsolete in which case I skip it. Otherwise, I output the initial part of the macro declaration up to the equal sign. From here on, I go different routes for the different types of declarations.

⟨ convert t from WEB to cweb 79 ⟩ +≡ (141)
case ATD:
$\quad$ {
$\quad\quad$ **token** $*eq = t{\rightarrow}next{\rightarrow}next;$
$\quad\quad \text{DBG}(dbgcweb, \texttt{"Macro␣definition␣in␣line␣\%d\textbackslash n"}, t{\rightarrow}lineno);$
$\quad\quad$ **if** $(\text{SYM}(t{\rightarrow}next){\rightarrow}obsolete)\ t = wskip\_to(t, eq{\rightarrow}link);$
$\quad\quad$ **else** {
$\quad\quad\quad wputs(\texttt{"@d␣"}), t = t{\rightarrow}next;\ wprint(\text{SYM}(t){\rightarrow}name);$
$\quad\quad\quad$ **if** $(t{\rightarrow}tag \equiv \text{NMACRO})$ ⟨ convert NMACRO from WEB to cweb 143 ⟩
$\quad\quad\quad$ **else if** $(t{\rightarrow}tag \equiv \text{OMACRO})$ ⟨ convert OMACRO from WEB to cweb 142 ⟩
$\quad\quad\quad$ **else if** $(t{\rightarrow}tag \equiv \text{PMACRO})$ ⟨ convert PMACRO from WEB to cweb 145 ⟩
$\quad\quad\quad$ **else** $\text{ERROR}(\texttt{"Macro␣name␣expected␣in␣line␣\%d"}, t{\rightarrow}lineno);$
$\quad\quad$ }
$\quad\quad \text{DBG}(dbgcweb, \texttt{"End␣Macro␣definition␣in␣line␣\%d\textbackslash n"}, t{\rightarrow}lineno);\ $ **break**;
$\quad$ }
case ATF:
$\quad$ {
$\quad\quad$ **token** $*eq = t{\rightarrow}next{\rightarrow}next;$
$\quad\quad \text{DBG}(dbgcweb, \texttt{"Format␣definition␣in␣line␣\%d\textbackslash n"}, t{\rightarrow}lineno);$
$\quad\quad$ **if** $(\text{SYM}(t{\rightarrow}next){\rightarrow}obsolete)\ t = wskip\_to(t, eq{\rightarrow}link);$
$\quad\quad$ **else** {
$\quad\quad\quad wputs(\texttt{"@f␣"}), t = t{\rightarrow}next;\ wprint(\text{SYM}(t){\rightarrow}name);$
$\quad\quad\quad t = wprint\_to(eq{\rightarrow}next, eq{\rightarrow}link);$
$\quad\quad$ }
$\quad\quad$ **break**;
$\quad$ }

Ordinary parameterless macros map directly to C style macros.

⟨ convert OMACRO from WEB to cweb 142 ⟩ ≡ (142)
$\quad$ {
$\quad\quad wput(\texttt{'\textbackslash t'});\ t = eq{\rightarrow}next;$

5.9 Macro and format declarations

}   Used in 141.

    WEB features numeric macros that are evaluated to a numeric value by WEB before they are inserted into the final Pascal program. When converting such macros to C style macros, I have to make sure that a replacement text containing operators is evaluated as one expression. For example when TEX defines $single\_base \equiv active\_base + 256$, where $active\_base \equiv 1$, then $print\_esc(p - single\_base)$ should be evaluated as $print\_esc(p - (1 + 256))$ not $print\_esc(p - 1 + 256)$. So I add an extra pair of parentheses around the replacement text in case it contains a plus sign or a minus sign.

⟨ convert NMACRO from WEB to cweb 143 ⟩ ≡   (143)
```
{
  int has_operators;
  wput('\t'); has_operators = 0;
  for (t = eq→next; t ≠ eq→link ∧ t→tag ≠ MLEFT ∧ t→tag ≠ NL;
       t = t→next)
    if (t→tag ≡ PPLUS ∨ t→tag ≡ PMINUS) {
      has_operators = 1; break; }
  if (has_operators) wput('(');
  for (t = eq→next; t ≠ eq→link ∧ t→tag ≠ MLEFT ∧ t→tag ≠ NL;
       t = wtoken(t)) continue;
  if (has_operators) wput(')');
}
```
                                                                                                                Used in 141.

    Parametrized macros in WEB can use any number of arguments. In C, typical parametrized macros have a fixed number of arguments, variadic macros being the exception rather than the rule. Therefore, I count the number of macro arguments each time I expand a macro. Since TEX uses macros with a fixed number of arguments only for 1, 2, or 3 arguments, I use the value 4, for variadic macros.

⟨ count macro parameters 144 ⟩ ≡   (144)
```
{
  token *p;
  int count = 1;
  if (open→next→tag ≡ HASH) {
    DBG(dbgmacro,"Counting %s parameters (#) in line %d\n",
        SYM(t)→name, t→lineno);
  }
  else {
    for (p = open→next; p ≠ open→link; p = p→next)
      if (p→tag ≡ PCOMMA) count++;
      else if (p→tag ≡ POPEN) p = p→link;
    if (SYM(t)→value ≡ 0) SYM(t)→value = count;
    else if (SYM(t)→value ≠ count) SYM(t)→value = 4;
    DBG(dbgmacro,"Counting %s parameters %d line %d\n",
        SYM(t)→name, SYM(t)→value, t→lineno);
  }
```

} Used in 90.

Now that I know the number of arguments, I can construct the macro definition.

⟨ convert PMACRO from WEB to cweb 145 ⟩ ≡ (145)
{
    static char $*params[4] = \{$"X"$,$ "X"$,$ "X,$\sqcup$Y"$,$ "X,$\sqcup$Y,$\sqcup$Z"$\};$
                          /* if I have no information, I assume 1 */
    char $*param;$
    $eq = eq \rightarrow next;$ /* account for the (#) token */
    if $(\text{SYM}(t) \rightarrow value > 3)$ {
        $param =$ "..."$;$ $hash\_str =$ "__VA_ARGS__"$;$ }
    else $hash\_str = param = params[\text{SYM}(t) \rightarrow value];$
    $wput(\text{'}(\text{'}), wputs(param), wputs(\text{"})\backslash\text{t"}), t = eq \rightarrow next;$
}
                                                                      Used in 141.

⟨ global variables 11 ⟩ +≡ (146)
    static char $*hash\_str;$

⟨ convert t from WEB to cweb 79 ⟩ +≡ (147)
case HASH: $wprint(hash\_str), t = t \rightarrow next;$ **break**;

5.10 Labels

In C, labels are identifiers and labels do not need a declaration. So in the parser, I mark the tokens belonging to a label declaration with the tag CIGNORE and they will be ignored when the cweb file is written.

The tag CLABEL is used now to mark the labels when they are used. In most cases the labels in TEX are numeric macros. So I use the name of the macro as the name of the CLABEL token and mark the definition of the numeric macro as obsolete (Occasionally these label names are modified by adding an integer). In the rare cases where the label is indeed an integer, I use the tag CLABELN. In this case I add the prefix "label" to the numeric value to make it a C identifier. Further, I count the number of times a label is used. Later transformation might render a label as unused and I can remove also the target label. The whole bookkeeping is achieved by calling the function *clabel* at appropriate places in the parser.

⟨ external declarations 5 ⟩ +≡ (148)
    extern void $clabel(\textbf{token} *t, \textbf{int} \ use);$

⟨ functions 13 ⟩ +≡ (149)
    void $clabel(\textbf{token} *t, \textbf{int} \ use)$
    {
        if $(t \rightarrow tag \equiv \text{NMACRO})$ {
            $\text{SYM}(t) \rightarrow obsolete = true;$ $\text{SYM}(t) \rightarrow value \mathrel{+}= use;$ $t \rightarrow tag = \text{CLABEL};$
        }
        else if $(t \rightarrow tag \equiv \text{CLABEL})$ $\text{SYM}(t) \rightarrow value \mathrel{+}= use;$
        else if $(t \rightarrow tag \equiv \text{PRETURN})$ $\text{SYM}(t) \rightarrow value \mathrel{+}= use;$
        else {
            if $(t \rightarrow tag \equiv \text{PINTEGER})$ $t \rightarrow tag = \text{CLABELN};$

5.10 Labels

```
      return;
    }
    DBG(dbgstring, "Using label %s (%d) in line %d\n", SYM(t)→name,
        SYM(t)→value, t→lineno);
}
```

A very special case is the **return** macro of TEX; it is defined as **goto** *exit*. I need to deal with it in a special way, because it usually follows the assignment of a function return value and therefore can be converted to a C **return** statement. In the scanner, I create the PRETURN token and set its symbol number to the *exit* symbol.

⟨ external declarations 5 ⟩ +≡ (150)
  extern int *exit_no*;
#**define** TOK_RETURN
  {
    token ∗*t* = *add_token*(PRETURN);
    t→*sym_no* = *exit_no*;
  }

⟨ global variables 11 ⟩ +≡ (151)
  int *exit_no*;

⟨ initialize token list 22 ⟩ +≡ (152)
  exit_no = *get_sym_no*("exit");

While parsing, I replace the symbol number by the symbol pointer to reflect local *exit* labels.

⟨ special treatment for WEB tokens 73 ⟩ +≡ (153)
case PRETURN: *t*→*sym_ptr* = SYM(*t*); *pp_stack*[*pp_sp*].*next* = *t*→*next*;
  goto *found*;

The output of the C-style labels is done with the following code. In the case of a CLABEL, I check the use-count in *value* and eliminate unused labels; I also check for a plus sign and a second number (remember labels in Pascal are numeric values) and if found append the number to the label name.

⟨ convert *t* from WEB to cweb 79 ⟩ +≡ (154)
case CLABEL:
  if (*t*→*sym_ptr*→*value* ≤ 0) {
    t = *t*→*next*;
    if (*t*→*tag* ≡ PPLUS) *t* = *t*→*next*→*next*;
    if (*t*→*tag* ≡ PCOLON) {
      t = *t*→*next*;
      if (*t*→*tag* ≡ CSEMICOLON) *t* = *t*→*next*;
    }
  }
  else {
    wprint(SYM(*t*)→*name*); *t* = *t*→*next*;
    if (*t*→*tag* ≡ PPLUS) {

$t = t{\rightarrow}next;\ \ wputs(t{\rightarrow}text);\ \ t = t{\rightarrow}next;$
   }
}
break;
case CLABELN: $wprint("\texttt{label}");\ wputs(t{\rightarrow}text);\ t = t{\rightarrow}next;$ **break**;
case PEXIT: $wprint("\texttt{exit(0)}");\ t = t{\rightarrow}next;$ **break**;
case PRETURN: $wprint("\texttt{goto\_end}");\ t = t{\rightarrow}next;$ **break**;

5.11 Constant declarations

In TEX there are only two types of constant declarations: integers and strings. I also observe, that the integer declarations are followed by at most one string declaration. While parsing, I change the tag of the identifier getting defined to CINTDEF or CSTRDEF. I convert the constant declarations into an enumeration type or a **const char** ∗.

⟨convert t from WEB to cweb 79⟩ +≡ (155)
case CINTDEF: $wputs("\texttt{enum\_\{@+}"),\ wid(t),\ wput('=');$
$t = wprint\_to(t{\rightarrow}link{\rightarrow}next, t{\rightarrow}link{\rightarrow}link);\ wputs("\texttt{@+\};}");\ t = t{\rightarrow}next;$
break;
case CSTRDEF: $wprint("\texttt{const\_char\_*}"),\ wid(t);\ t = t{\rightarrow}next;$ **break**;

I have used above a technique that I will use often in the following code. While parsing, I use the link filed of the tokens to connect key tokens of a certain Pascal constructions. Using these links, I can find the different parts (including the intervening WEB tokens) and rearrange them as needed. Linking tokens is achieved with the following macro which also checks that the link stays within the same code sequence.

⟨external declarations 5⟩ +≡ (156)
#**define** LNK($from, to$) (($from$) ? ($seq((from), (to)), (from){\rightarrow}link = (to))$: 0)

5.12 Variable declarations

When I parse variable declarations, I replace the *tag* of the first variable identifier by PDEFVARID and link all the variables following it together. The last variable is linked to the token separating the identifier from the type, a PCOLON token which the parser has changed to a CIGNORE token. The former PCOLON token itself is then linked to the PSEMICOLON that terminates the variable declaration. In the special case of array variables, I have to insert the variable identifiers inside the type definition. To accomplish this, I set the global variable *varlist* to point to the PDEFVARID token, and continue after printing the type with whatever is left from this list. Note the special precautions taken to get the type of variables right that are used to control **for**-loops; I deal with this problem in section 5.16.

⟨internal declarations 3⟩ +≡ (157)
   static token ∗*varlist*;

⟨global variables 11⟩ +≡ (158)
   static token ∗*varlist* = NULL;

Using this information I can convert the variable declaration.

5.13 Types

⟨ convert t from WEB to cweb 79 ⟩ +≡ (159)
case PDEFVARID:
{
   token *$type = t\rightarrow link$;
   $varlist = t$;
   DBG($dbgcweb$, "Converting␣variable␣list␣in␣line␣%d\n", $t\rightarrow lineno$);
   while ($type\rightarrow tag \equiv$ PID) $type = type\rightarrow link$;
   {
     int $replace = 0$;
     ⟨ decide whether to replace a subrange type for loop control variables 184 ⟩
     if ($replace$) {
       $wprint$("int");
       DBG($dbgfor$, "\tReplacing␣subrange␣type␣by␣int\n");
     }
     else $wprint\_to(type, type\rightarrow link)$;
   }
   DBG($dbgcweb$, "Finished␣variable␣type␣in␣line␣%d\n", $t\rightarrow lineno$);
   if ($varlist\rightarrow tag \equiv$ PDEFVARID) {
     $wid(varlist)$; $varlist = varlist\rightarrow next$; }
   $wprint\_to(varlist, type)$; $t = type\rightarrow link$;
   DBG($dbgcweb$, "Finishing␣variable␣list␣in␣line␣%d\n", $t\rightarrow lineno$);
   break;
}

5.13 Types

Pascal type declarations start with the keyword **type**, then follows a list of declarations each one starting with a type identifier. While parsing Pascal, I change the *tag* of the identifier being defined to PDEFTYPEID. I link this token to the first token of the type, and link the first token of the type to the semicolon terminating the type. When I encounter these *tags* now a second time, I can convert them into C **typedef**'s.

⟨ convert t from WEB to cweb 79 ⟩ +≡ (160)
case PDEFTYPEID:
{
   token *$type\_name = t$;
   token *$type = type\_name\rightarrow link$;
   DBG($dbgcweb$, "Defining␣type␣%s␣in␣line␣%d\n", $token2string(t)$,
      $t\rightarrow lineno$); $wprint$("typedef␣"); $t = wprint\_to(type, type\rightarrow link)$;
   $wprint(token2string(type\_name))$; **break**;
}

The above code just uses $wprint\_to$ to print the type itself. Some types need a little help to print correctly. For instance, subrange types are converted by changing the PEQ token after the new type identifier to a CTSUBRANGE token, with an *up*-link to the parse tree for the subrange. Since C does not have this kind of subrange types, I approximate them by the standard integer types found in stdint.h.

⟨ convert t from WEB to cweb 79 ⟩ +≡ (161)
case CTSUBRANGE:
{
    int $lo = t{\rightarrow}up{\rightarrow}previous{\rightarrow}value$;
    int $hi = t{\rightarrow}up{\rightarrow}next{\rightarrow}value$;
    DBG($dbgcweb$, "Defining␣subrange␣type␣%d..%d\n", lo, hi);
    if ($lo < 0 \wedge$ INT8_MIN $\leq lo \wedge hi \leq$ INT8_MAX) $wprint$("int8_t");
    else if ($0 \leq lo \wedge hi \leq$ UINT8_MAX) $wprint$("uint8_t");
    else if ($lo < 0 \wedge$ INT16_MIN $\leq lo \wedge hi \leq$ INT16_MAX) $wprint$("int16_t");
    else if ($0 \leq lo \wedge hi \leq$ UINT16_MAX) $wprint$("uint16_t");
    else if ($lo < 0 \wedge$ INT32_MIN $\leq lo \wedge hi \leq$ INT32_MAX) $wprint$("int32_t");
    else if ($0 \leq lo \wedge hi \leq$ UINT32_MAX) $wprint$("uint32_t");
    else ERROR("unable␣to␣convert␣subrange␣type␣%d..%d␣in␣line␣%d\n",
        $lo, hi, t{\rightarrow}lineno$);
    $t = t{\rightarrow}link$; **break**;
}

To set *up*-links in the parser, I use the following macro:

⟨ external declarations 5 ⟩ +≡ (162)
#define UP($from, to$) (($from$)${\rightarrow}up = (to)$)

Record types get converted into C structures; the variant parts of records become C unions.

⟨ convert t from WEB to cweb 79 ⟩ +≡ (163)
case PRECORD:
{
    DBG($dbgcweb$, "Converting␣record␣type␣in␣line␣%d\n", $t{\rightarrow}lineno$);
    $wprint$("struct␣{␣"); $t = wprint\_to(t{\rightarrow}next, t{\rightarrow}link)$;
    DBG($dbgcweb$, "Finished␣record␣type␣in␣line␣%d\n", $t{\rightarrow}lineno$);
    $wprint$("}␣"); **break**;
}
case CUNION:
{
    DBG($dbgcweb$, "Converting␣union␣type␣in␣line␣%d\n", $t{\rightarrow}lineno$);
    $wprint$("union␣{␣"); $t = wprint\_to(t{\rightarrow}next, t{\rightarrow}link)$; $wprint$("};");
    DBG($dbgcweb$, "Finished␣union␣type␣in␣line␣%d\n", $t{\rightarrow}lineno$); **break**;
}

The conversion of the field declarations of a record type assumes that the Pascal parser has changed the first PID token to a PDEFVARID token and linked it to the following PCOLON token; then linked the PCOLON token to the PSEMICOLON or PEND token that follows the type.

Arrays also need special conversion. Pascal arrays specify a subrange type while C arrays are always zero based and specify a size. Common to both is the specification

5.13 Types

of an element type. TEX does not use named array types. Array types only occur in the definition of variables.

I link the PARRAY token to the PSQOPEN token, which I link to either the PDOTDOT token or the type identifier, which I link to the PSQCLOSE token, which I link to the POF token, which is finally linked to the PSEMICOLON following the element type.

The *up* pointer of the PARRAY token points to the parse tree for the subrange of the index type.

⟨convert t from WEB to cweb 79⟩ +≡   (164)
```
case PARRAY:
  if (t→up ≡ NULL)
              /* happens for example code which is not part of the program */
    wputs(t→text), t = t→next;
  else {
    token *from = t→link;
    token *index = from→link;
    token *to = index→link;
    token *element_type = to→link;
    token *subrange = t→up;
    int lo, hi, zero_based;

    if (subrange→tag ≡ PID) subrange = subrange→sym_ptr→type;
    lo = subrange→previous→value;
    hi = subrange→next→value; zero_based = (subrange→previous→tag ≡
        PINTEGER ∧ lo ≡ 0) ∨ subrange→previous→tag ≡ PTYPECHAR;
    DBG(dbgarray, "Converting␣array[%d..%d]␣type␣in␣line␣%d\n", lo, hi,
        t→lineno); t = wprint_to(element_type, element_type→link);
    while (true) {
      CHECK(varlist ≠ NULL,
          "Nonempty␣variable␣list␣expected␣in␣line␣%d", varlist→lineno);
      DBG(dbgarray, "Generating␣array␣variable␣%s␣in␣line␣%d\n",
          varlist→sym_ptr→name, varlist→lineno); wid(varlist);
      if (¬zero_based) wput('0');           /* add a zero to the array name */
      wput('['); ⟨generate array size 165⟩ wput(']');
      if (¬zero_based)   /* now I need the array with the appropriate offset */
      {
        DBG(dbgarray,
            "Generating␣array␣pointer␣%s[%s=%d..␣]␣in␣line␣%d\n",
            varlist→sym_ptr→name, token2string(from→next), lo,
            varlist→lineno); wputs(",␣*const␣"); wid(varlist);
        wputs("␣=␣"); wid(varlist), wput('0'); ⟨generate array offset 166⟩;
      }
      varlist = varlist→link;
      if (varlist→tag ≡ PDEFVARID ∨ varlist→tag ≡ PID) wput(',');
      else break;
    }
```

```
    DBG(dbgarray,"Finished␣array␣type␣in␣line␣%d\n",t→lineno);
}
break;
```
⟨ generate array size 165 ⟩ ≡ (165)
```
{
  int hi, size;
  hi = generate_constant(subrange→next, 0, 0);
  size = generate_constant(subrange→previous, '-', hi);  size = size + 1;
  if (size < 0) wput('-'), wputi(−size);
  else if (size > 0) {
    if (subrange→previous→tag ≠ PTYPECHAR ∧ (subrange→previous→tag ≠
        PINTEGER ∨ subrange→next→tag ≠ PINTEGER)) wput('+');
    wputi(size);
  }
}
```
Used in 164.

⟨ generate array offset 166 ⟩ ≡ (166)
```
{
  int lo = generate_constant(subrange→previous, '-', 0);
  if (lo < 0) wput('-'), wputi(−lo);
  else if (lo > 0) wput('+'), wputi(lo);
}
```
Used in 164.

I use the following function to generate a symbolic expression for the given parse tree representing a constant integer value. The expression contains only plus or minus operators. Parentheses are eliminated using the *sign* parameter. The function returns the numeric value that needs to be printed after all the symbolic constants, accumulating literal constants on its way.

⟨ functions 13 ⟩ +≡ (167)
```
  int generate_constant(token *t, char sign, int value)
  {
    if (t→tag ≡ PTYPECHAR ∨ t→tag ≡ PINTEGER) {
      if (sign ≡ '-') return value − t→value;
      else return value + t→value;
    }
    else if (t→tag ≡ NMACRO ∨ t→tag ≡ PCONSTID) {
      if (sign ≠ 0) wput(sign);
      wprint(token2string(t→previous));  return value;
    }
    if (t→tag ≡ PPLUS) {
      if (t→previous ≠ NULL)
        value = generate_constant(t→previous, sign, value);
      if (sign ≡ 0) sign = '+';
      return generate_constant(t→next, sign, value);
    }
    if (t→tag ≡ PMINUS) {
```

5.15 Structured statements

```
        if (t→previous ≠ NULL)
            value = generate_constant(t→previous, sign, value);
        if (sign ≡ 0 ∨ sign ≡ '+') sign = '-';
        else sign = '+';
        return generate_constant(t→next, sign, value);
    }
    else ERROR("Unexpected␣tag␣%s␣while␣generating␣a␣co\
        nstant␣expression␣in␣line␣%d", TAG(t), t→lineno);
}
```

⟨internal declarations 3⟩ +≡ (168)
   int *generate_constant*(**token** ∗*t*, **char** *sign*, **int** *value*);

5.14 Files

The Pascal idea of a file, let's say "*fmt_file*: **file of** *memory_word*", is a combination of two things: the file itself and the file's buffer variable capable of holding one data item, in this case one *memory_word*. In C, I can simulate such a Pascal file by a structure containing both: **FILE** ∗*f*, the file in the C sense; and *memory_word d*, the data item.

⟨convert *t* from WEB to cweb 79⟩ +≡ (169)
case PFILE:
```
    {
        DBG(dbgcweb, "Converting␣file␣type␣in␣line␣%d\n", t→lineno);
        wprint("struct␣{@+FILE␣*f;@+"); t = wprint_to(t→next, t→link);
        wprint("@,d;@+}␣");
        DBG(dbgcweb, "Finished␣file␣type␣in␣line␣%d\n", t→lineno); break;
    }
```

As I will show in section 5.18, it is also convenient that TEX always passes files, and only files, by reference to functions or procedures. Now I can transcribe *get*(*fmt_file*) into *fread*(&*fmt_file.d*, **sizeof** (*memory_word*), 1, *fmt_file.f*). I put these "rewrite rules" as macros in the patch file; it has the advantage that the rewriting does not disturb the visual appearance of the program code.

Access to the file's buffer variable, in Pascal written as *f*ˆ becomes simply *f.d*.

⟨convert *t* from WEB to cweb 79⟩ +≡ (170)
case PUP: *wputs*(".d"); *t* = *t*→*next*; **break**;

5.15 Structured statements

Some of the structured statements are easy to convert. For example the **if** statement just needs an extra pair of parentheses around the controlling expression. These small adjustment are made when dealing with the PIF and PTHEN token. The **while** statement is similarly simple, but the PDO token may also be part of a **for**-loop. So the parser links the PWHILE token to the PDO token to insert the parentheses.

⟨convert *t* from WEB to cweb 79⟩ +≡ (171)
case PWHILE: *wprint*("while␣");

if $(t{\to}link \neq \text{NULL})$ {
    $wput(\text{'('}); \; t = wprint\_to(t{\to}next, t{\to}link); \; wputs(\text{") "});$
}
$t = t{\to}next;$ **break**;

Other structured statements need more work.

Let's start with the Pascal **case** statement. Adding parentheses around the controlling expression is not as simple, because I lack a unique second keyword; instead I have a POF token which occurs at various places and is usually ignored. So I link the PCASE token to the corresponding POF token while parsing and generate a **switch** statement.

⟨ convert t from WEB to cweb 79 ⟩ +≡   (172)
case PCASE:
    if $(t{\to}link \equiv \text{NULL})$ {
        $wprint(t{\to}text); \; t = t{\to}next;$
    }
    else {
        $wprint(\text{"switch ("}); \; t = wprint\_to(t{\to}next, t{\to}link); \; wputs(\text{") \{"});$
    }
    break;

The case labels are converted while parsing. While Pascal requires a list of labels followed by a semicolon and a statement, C needs the keyword "**case**" preceding a single label, a colon, and a statement list usually ending with "**break**;". When faced with this problem, I tried a new strategy: inserting new tokens. I insert a CCASE token before each Pascal case label and replace the PCOMMA between labels by a CCOLON. (While it worked quite well, I still wished, I would have solved the problem without modifying the token list).

To insert the CCASE tokens, the parser uses the function *winsert_after*.

⟨ external declarations 5 ⟩ +≡   (173)
    extern token *$*winsert\_after$(**token** $*t$, **int** tag, **char** $*text$);

⟨ functions 13 ⟩ +≡   (174)
    token $*winsert\_after$(**token** $*t$, **int** tag, **char** $*text$)
    {
        token $*n$;
        $\text{DBG}(dbgcweb, \text{"Inserting token \%s after \%s in line \%d\textbackslash n"},$
            $tagname(tag), \text{TAG}(t), t{\to}lineno); \; n = new\_token(tag);$
        $n{\to}next = t{\to}next; \; n{\to}next{\to}previous = n; \; n{\to}previous = t; \; t{\to}next = n;$
        $n{\to}sequenceno = t{\to}sequenceno; \; n{\to}lineno = t{\to}lineno; \; n{\to}text = text;$
        return n;
    }

Further, the parser replaces the semicolons separating the Pascal case elements by a CBREAK token.

⟨ convert t from WEB to cweb 79 ⟩ +≡   (175)
case CBREAK:

5.15 Structured statements

```
if (t→previous→tag ≠ PSEMICOLON ∧ t→previous→tag ≠
    CSEMICOLON ∧ t→previous→tag ≠ PEND) wputs("@;");
if (¬dead_end(t→up,t→lineno)) wprint("@+break;");
t = t→next;  break;
```

The semicolon that might be necessary before the "**break**" is inserted using a general procedure described in section 5.17.

TEX often terminates the statement following the case label with a **goto** statement. In this case of course it looks silly to add a **break** statement. I can test this by calling the *dead_end* function

⟨ external declarations 5 ⟩ +≡   (176)
    int *dead_end*(**token** *t*, **int** *lineno*);

⟨ functions 13 ⟩ +≡   (177)
```
int dead_end(token *t, int lineno)
{
  DBG(dbgbreak,"Searching for dead end in line %d:\n",lineno);
  while (true) {
    DBG(dbgbreak,"\t%s\n",TAG(t));
    if (t→tag ≡ PGOTO ∨ t→tag ≡ PEXIT ∨ t→tag ≡ CPROCRETURN)
      return true;
    else if (t→tag ≡ PCOLON)  t = t→next;
    else if (t→tag ≡ PBEGIN)  t = t→previous;
    else if (t→tag ≡ PSEMICOLON ∨ t→tag ≡ CCASE) {
      if (t→next→tag ≡ CEMPTY)  t = t→previous;
      else  t = t→next;
    }
    else return false;
  }
}
```

The "**others**" label can be replaced by "**default**".

⟨ convert *t* from WEB to cweb 79 ⟩ +≡   (178)
   case POTHERS: *wprint*("default:"); *t* = *t*→*next*; **break**;

I suspect that a *case_list* always ends with either a semicolon or POTHERS without a semicolon. It could be better to generate also a **break** statement at the end of the last case element—especially if the order of cases gets rearranged by rearranging or adding modules.

Finally I convert the **repeat**-**until** statement. The "**repeat**" becomes "**do {**" and the "**until**" becomes "**} while**". All that is left is to enclose the expression following the "**until**" in a pair of parentheses and add a ¬ operator. The opening parenthesis follows the "**while**"; but where should the closing parenthesis's go? Here I use the fact that in TEX the condition after the "**until**" is either followed directly by a semicolon, or by the start of a new section.

⟨ convert *t* from WEB to cweb 79 ⟩ +≡   (179)
   case PREPEAT: *wprint*("@/do@+{"); *t* = *t*→*next*; **break**;
   case PUNTIL:

{
  int *sequenceno*, *lineno*;
  token *∗end*;
  wputs("}@+␣while␣(!("); *sequenceno* = *t*→*sequenceno*;
  lineno = *t*→*lineno*; *end* = *t*→*next*;
  while (*true*) {
    if (*end*→*tag* ≡ PSEMICOLON ∨ *end*→*tag* ≡ CSEMICOLON ∨ *end*→*tag* ≡
        PELSE) **break**;
    else if (*end*→*tag* ≡ ATSPACE) {
      while (*true*) {
        int *tag* = *end*→*previous*→*tag*;
        if (*tag* > FIRST_PASCAL_TOKEN ∨ *tag* ≡ OMACRO ∨ *tag* ≡
            NMACRO ∨ *tag* ≡ CHAR) **break**;
        end = *end*→*previous*;
      }
      break;
    }
    end = *end*→*next*;
  }
  CHECK(*sequenceno* ≡ *end*→*sequenceno*,
      "until:␣end␣of␣expression␣not␣found␣in␣line␣%d", *lineno*);
  t = *wprint_to*(*t*→*next*, *end*); *wputs*(")"); **break**;
}

5.16 for-loops

To convert the **for** statement, I link the PFOR token to the PTO or PDOWNTO token respectively, which is then linked to the PDO token. The rest seems simple but it hides a surprising difficulty.

⟨ convert *t* from WEB to cweb 79 ⟩ +≡   (180)
case PFOR:
  {
    token *∗id* = *t*→*next*;
    token *∗to* = *t*→*link*;
    if (*to* ≡ NULL) {
      wprint("for"); *t* = *t*→*next*; **break**;
    }
    wprint("for␣("); *wprint_to*(*id*, *to*); *wputs*(";␣"); *wid*(*id*);
    if (*to*→*tag* ≡ PTO) *wputs*("<=");
    else if (*to*→*tag* ≡ PDOWNTO) *wputs*(">=");
    else ERROR("to␣or␣downto␣expected␣in␣line␣%d", *to*→*lineno*);
    wprint_to(*to*→*next*, *to*→*link*); *wputs*(";␣"); *wid*(*id*);
    if (*to*→*tag* ≡ PTO) *wputs*("++");
    else *wputs*("--");
    wputs(")␣"); *t* = *to*→*link*→*next*; **break**;

5.16 for-loops

}

The above code checks that there is actually a link to the PTO token. This link will exist only if the **for**-loop was parsed as part of the Pascal program; it will not exists if the code segment was just part of an explanation (see for example section 823). In this case, I need to deal with the PTO and PDO separately.

Given a Pascal variable "**var** i: 0..255;" the **for**-loop "**for** $i := 255$ **downto** 0 **do**..." will work as expected. If I translate the variable definition to "**uint8_t** i;" the translated **for**-loop "**for** $(i = 255;\ i \geq 0;\ i\text{--})$..." will not terminate because the loop control variable will never be smaller than 0, instead it will wrap around. If the variable i is used in such a **for**-loop, I should define it simply as "**int** i;".

The first step is the analysis of **for**-loops in the Pascal parser. To do so, I call the function *mark_for_variable* with three parameters: *id*, the loop control variable; *lineno*, the line number for debugging purposes; *value*, the value of the limit terminating the loop; and *direction*, indicating the type of loop. For the *direction*, I distinguish three cases: TO_LOOP, DOWNTO_LOOP, and loops where the loops limit is a variable (VAR_LOOP).

⟨ external declarations 5 ⟩ +≡   (181)
#**define** VAR_LOOP 0
#**define** TO_LOOP   1
#**define** DOWNTO_LOOP 2

The function then tries to decide whether the type of the for loop control variable should be changed from a subrange type to a plain integer.

If the limit controlling the loop is a variable, I can not ensure (without reasoning about program semantics) that the limit will not coincide with the limit of the subrange type of the control variable. In this case I stay on the safe side and replace the subrange type.

If the limit controlling the loop is a constant, I check its value and replace the type of the control variable only if the value coincides with the upper (or lower) limit of the subrange type used for the control variable. The comparison of the given loop limit with the variables possible range limit is postponed until I generate the variable declaration. For now, I just determine the minimum number of *bits* needed for a suitable variable type.

⟨ functions 13 ⟩ +≡   (182)
  void *mark_for_variable*(**token** **id*, **int** *lineno*, **int** *value*, **int** *direction*)
  {
    int *replace* = 0;
    int *bits* = 0;

    if (*direction* ≡ VAR_LOOP) *replace* = 1;
    else if (*direction* ≡ DOWNTO_LOOP) {
      if (*value* ≥ 0) *bits* = 0;   /* lower limit of all unsigned types */
      else if (*value* > INT8_MIN) *bits* = 6;
      else if (*value* > INT16_MIN) *bits* = 14;
      else *bits* = 15;
    }

```
    else                                                    /* TO_LOOP */
    {
      if (value < 0) bits = 0;
      else if (value < INT8_MAX) bits = 6;
      else if (value < UINT8_MAX) bits = 7;
      else if (value < INT16_MAX) bits = 14;
      else if (value < UINT16_MAX) bits = 15;
      else if (value < INT32_MAX) bits = 31;
      else bits = 32;
    }
    SYM(id)→for_ctrl = FOR_CTRL_PACK(lineno, replace, direction, bits);
}
```

I pack the result of my analysis into the *for_ctrl* field of the variables symbol table entry using the following macros.

⟨ external declarations 5 ⟩ +≡   (183)
  extern void *mark_for_variable*(**token** **id*, **int** *lineno*, **int** *value*, **int** *direction*);
#**define** FOR_CTRL_PACK(*lineno, replace, direction, bits*)
  ((*lineno* ≪ 16) | ((*replace* & #1) ≪ 15) | ((*direction* & #3) ≪ 13) | (*bits* & #1FFF))
#**define** FOR_CTRL_LINE(*X*)   (((*X*) ≫ 16) & #FFFF)
#**define** FOR_CTRL_REPLACE(*X*)   (((*X*) ≫ 15) & 1)
#**define** FOR_CTRL_DIRECTION(*X*)   (((*X*) ≫ 13) & #3)
#**define** FOR_CTRL_BITS(*X*)   ((*X*) & #1FFF)

When I finally come to the place where I generate a variable declaration, I can decide whether to replace a subrange type for loop control variables. To do this I iterate over the list of variables and if I find in the list one variable that requires replacement, I change the type of the whole list (this is a bit more than necessary, but it does no harm either).

⟨ decide whether to replace a subrange type for loop control variables 184 ⟩ ≡ (184)
```
{
  token *subrange = NULL;
  if (type→tag ≡ CTSUBRANGE) subrange = type→up;
  else if (type→tag ≡ CIGNORE ∧ type→next→tag ≡
           PID ∧ type→next→sym_ptr→type ≠
           NULL ∧ type→next→sym_ptr→type→tag ≡ PDOTDOT)
    subrange = type→next→sym_ptr→type;     /* subrange type identifier */
  if (subrange ≠ NULL) {
    token *id = t;
    while (id ≠ type ∧ ¬replace) {
      if (id→sym_ptr→for_ctrl ≠ 0) {
        int lo = subrange→previous→value;
        int hi = subrange→next→value;
        int bits = FOR_CTRL_BITS(id→sym_ptr→for_ctrl);
        int direction = FOR_CTRL_DIRECTION(id→sym_ptr→for_ctrl);
        int lineno = FOR_CTRL_LINE(id→sym_ptr→for_ctrl);
```

$replace = $ FOR_CTRL_REPLACE$(id\rightarrow sym\_ptr\rightarrow for\_ctrl)$;
DBG$(dbgfor,$ "Subrange␣for␣marked␣variable␣%s␣in␣line␣%d\n",
    $token2string(id), id\rightarrow lineno)$;
DBG$(dbgfor,$ "\tRange␣%d␣to␣%d,␣limit␣%d␣bits,␣direct\
    ion␣%d␣in␣line␣%d\n", $lo, hi, bits, direction, lineno)$;
if $(direction \equiv $ DOWNTO_LOOP$)$ {
  if $(lo \geq 0 \wedge bits \equiv 0)$ $replace = true$;
  else if $(lo < 0 \wedge $ INT8_MIN $\leq lo \wedge hi \leq $ INT8_MAX $\wedge bits \geq 7)$
    $replace = true$;
  else if $(lo < 0 \wedge $ INT16_MIN $\leq lo \wedge hi \leq $ INT16_MAX $\wedge bits \geq 15)$
    $replace = true$;
}
else if $(direction \equiv $ TO_LOOP$)$ {
  if $(lo < 0 \wedge $ INT8_MIN $\leq lo \wedge hi \leq $ INT8_MAX $\wedge bits \geq 7)$
    $replace = true$;
  else if $(0 \leq lo \wedge hi \leq $ UINT8_MAX $\wedge bits \geq 8)$ $replace = true$;
  else if $(lo < 0 \wedge $ INT16_MIN $\leq lo \wedge hi \leq $ INT16_MAX $\wedge bits \geq 15)$
    $replace = true$;
  else if $(0 \leq lo \wedge hi \leq $ UINT16_MAX $\wedge bits \geq 16)$ $replace = true$;
}
}
$id = id\rightarrow link$;
}
}
}

Used in 159.

5.17 Semicolons

In C, the semicolon is used to turn an expression, for example an assignment, into a statement; while in Pascal semicolons are used to separate statements in a statement sequence. This difference is important, because C will need in certain cases, for example, preceding an "**else**" or a "}" a semicolon, where Pascal must not have one.

The simpler case is the semicolon that in Pascal quite frequently follows an **end**. In C this semicolon often does no harm (it indicates an empty statement), but looks kind of strange, in other cases, for example following a procedure body, it must be eliminated. So I test for it and eliminate it wherever I find it.

⟨ convert t from WEB to cweb 79 ⟩ +≡ (185)
case PEND: $wputs($"}␣"$), t = t\rightarrow next$;
  if $(t\rightarrow tag \equiv $ PSEMICOLON$)$ $t = t\rightarrow next$;
  break;

Now let's turn to the more difficult case where C needs a semicolon and Pascal does not have one: preceding an "**else**", at the end of a *case_element*, and at the end of a statement sequence (preceding an "**end**" or "**until**"). Adding a semicolon directly before such an "**else**" would in many cases not look very nice. For instance when the code preceding it is in a different module. The semicolon should instead follow immediately after the last preceding Pascal token. I insert a CSEMICOLON token just there using the function *wsemicolon*. The function has two parameters: *t*, the token that might require a preceding semicolon; and *p*, the pointer to the parse tree preceding the token pointed to by *t*.

I first check the parse tree whether a semicolon is indeed needed, and if so, I search for the proper place to insert the semicolon. The function *wneeds_semicolon* descends into the parse tree, finds its rightmost statement, and determines whether it needs a semicolon. The function *wback* searches backward to the earliest token that is relevant for the C parser.

The situation is slightly different for ctangle. Its pattern matching algorithm does not work good, if the material, for example preceding an else, does not look like a statement, for example because the closing semicolon is hidden in a module or a macro. In these cases it is appropriate to insert a "@;" token. I do this by looking at the token preceding the "**else**", skipping over index entries, newlines, indents and such stuff, until finding the end of a module, or macro and insert the "@;" there.

⟨ functions 13 ⟩ +≡ (186)
  bool *wneeds_semicolon*(**token** *∗p*)
  {
    while ($p \neq$ NULL) {
      switch ($p \to tag$) {
      case PCASE: **case** PBEGIN: **case** CIGNORE: **return** *false*;
      case PSEMICOLON: **case** CCASE: **case** PELSE: $p = p \to next$; **continue**;
      case PIF: **case** PWHILE: **case** PFOR: **case** PCOLON:
        $p = p \to previous$; **continue**;
      case PASSIGN: **case** PFUNCID: **case** PCALLID: **case** PREPEAT:
        case PRETURN: **case** CRETURN: **case** CPROCRETURN: **case** PGOTO:
        case PEXIT: **case** CEMPTY: **default**: **return** *true*;
      }
    }
    return *false*;
  }
  static token *∗wback*(**token** *∗t*)
  {
    while (*true*) {
      CHECK($t \to previous \neq$ NULL, "Error␣searching␣backward");
      $t = t \to previous$;
      switch ($t \to tag$) {
      case PSEMICOLON: **case** CSEMICOLON: **case** PEND: **return** *t*;
      case RIGHT:
        while ($t \to tag \neq$ PLEFT $\wedge$ $t \to tag \neq$ MLEFT) $t = t \to previous$;
        break;
      case ATGREATER: **case** EQ: **case** HASH: **case** ATDOLLAR:
        case NMACRO: **case** OMACRO: **case** OCTAL: **case** HEX: **case** CHAR:
        case STRING: **case** PRETURN: **case** CEMPTY: **return** *t*;

5.17 Semicolons

```
      case CIGNORE: continue;
      default: break;
    }
    if (t→tag > FIRST_PASCAL_TOKEN) return t;
  }
}
void wsemicolon(token *p, token *t)
{
  t = wback(t);
  if (t→tag ≠ PSEMICOLON ∧ t→tag ≠ CSEMICOLON ∧ t→tag ≠ PEND) {
    if (wneeds_semicolon(p)) {
      DBG(dbgsemicolon, "inserting ; in line %d\n", t→lineno);
      if (t→next→tag ≡ ATSEMICOLON) {
        t→next→tag = CSEMICOLON;  t→next→text = ";";
      }
      else winsert_after(t, CSEMICOLON, ";");
    }
    else if (t→next→tag ≠ ATSEMICOLON ∧ t→next→tag ≠ PSEMICOLON) {
      DBG(dbgsemicolon, "inserting @; in line %d\n", t→lineno);
      winsert_after(t, ATSEMICOLON, "@;");
    }
  }
}
```

In procedures, I eliminate a final "*exit:*" because I have replaced "**goto** *exit*" by "**return**".

⟨ functions 13 ⟩ +≡   (187)
```
  void wend(token *p, token *t)
  {
    if (p→tag ≡ PSEMICOLON ∧ p→next→tag ≡
        PCOLON ∧ p→next→next→tag ≡ CEMPTY ∧ p→next→previous→tag ≡
        CLABEL ∧ p→next→previous→sym_no ≡ exit_no) {
      token *label = p→next→previous;
      DBG(dbgreturn, "Trailing exit: found preceding line %d\n",
          t→lineno);  label→tag = CIGNORE;  SYM(label)→value = −1000;
      CHECK(label→next→tag ≡ PCOLON,
            "Expected colon after label in line %d\n", label→lineno);
      label→next→tag = CIGNORE;  p→next→tag = CIGNORE;
    }
    else DBG(dbgreturn, "No trailing exit: found preceding line %d\n",
             t→lineno);
  }
```

⟨ external declarations 5 ⟩ +≡   (188)
```
  extern void wsemicolon(token *p, token *t);
  extern void wend(token *p, token *t);
```

The inserted semicolons have the tag CSEMICOLON. These tokens are printed but—and this is new—hidden from the Pascal parser. This idea might be useful also for other inserted tokens.

⟨convert token t to a string 39⟩ +≡ (189)
case CSEMICOLON: **return** ";";

⟨special treatment for WEB tokens 73⟩ +≡ (190)
case CSEMICOLON: $t = t{\rightarrow}next$; **continue**;

5.18 Procedures

While parsing, I link the PPROCEDURE token to the PSEMICOLON or POPEN following the procedure name. The PSEMICOLON following the heading is always changed to a CIGNORE.

⟨convert t from WEB to cweb 79⟩ +≡ (191)
case PPROCEDURE:
 DBG($dbgcweb$, "Converting␣procedure␣heading␣in␣line␣%d\n", $t{\rightarrow}lineno$);
 $wprint$("void"); $t = wprint\_to(t{\rightarrow}next, t{\rightarrow}link)$;
 if $(t{\rightarrow}tag \neq$ POPEN$)$ $wputs$("(void)");
 break;

The list of parameter identifiers spans from the beginning parenthesis that is pointed to by t to the closing parenthesis pointed to by $t{\rightarrow}link$. It is handled similar to a variable declaration. The type identifier, however, needs to be repeated for each parameter in a list. The parser has converted the parameter identifiers to either PDEFPARAMID or PDEFREFID, linked the identifiers together with the final link pointing to the PCOLON preceding the type, and it linked the PCOLON to the PSEMICOLON or PCLOSE following the type. This information is sufficient to convert the parameter list.

⟨convert t from WEB to cweb 79⟩ +≡ (192)
case PDEFPARAMID: **case** PDEFREFID:
 {
  token $*varlist = t$, $*type = t{\rightarrow}link$;
  DBG($dbgcweb$, "Converting␣parameter␣list␣in␣line␣%d\n", $t{\rightarrow}lineno$);
  while $(type{\rightarrow}tag \equiv$ PDEFPARAMID $\lor$ $type{\rightarrow}tag \equiv$ PDEFREFID$)$
   $type = type{\rightarrow}link$;
  while $(true)$ {
   $wprint\_to(type, type{\rightarrow}link)$;
   if $(varlist{\rightarrow}tag \equiv$ PDEFREFID$)$ $wputs$("␣*");
   $wid(varlist)$; $varlist = varlist{\rightarrow}link$;
   if $(varlist \neq type)$ $wput(',')$;
   else break;
  }
  $t = type{\rightarrow}link$;
  DBG($dbgcweb$, "Finishing␣parameter␣list␣in␣line␣%d\n", $t{\rightarrow}lineno$);
  break;
 }

5.18 Procedures

The parser changes the use of a reference variable to a CREFID token, and when I find one now, I dereference it.

⟨ convert t from WEB to cweb 79 ⟩ +≡ (193)
case CREFID: $wputs("(*"), wid(t), wput(')')$; $t = t{\rightarrow}next$; **break**;

Now consider a procedure call. The most complex part about it is the argument list. If a procedure has no parameters, there is no argument list in Pascal but there is an empty argument list in C. Further, the use of reference parameters complicates the processing. I need to add a "&" in front of a variable that is passed by reference in C. To accomplish this, the parser constructs for every procedure a *param_mask* and stores it in the *value* field of the procedure identifiers entry in the symbol table. A value of 1 means "no parameter list"; all the other bits correspond from left to right to up to 31 parameters; a bit is set if the corresponding parameter is a reference parameter. I use these definitions:

⟨ external declarations 5 ⟩ +≡ (194)
 extern unsigned int *param_mask*, *param_bit*;
#**define** SIGN_BIT $(\sim(((\textbf{unsigned int})\sim 0) \gg 1))$
#**define** START_PARAM $(param\_mask = 0, param\_bit = \text{SIGN\_BIT})$
#**define** NEXT_PARAM
   $(param\_bit = param\_bit \gg 1, \text{CHECK}(param\_bit \neq 0, "Too_\sqcup many_\sqcup parameters"))$
#**define** REF_PARAM $(param\_mask = param\_mask \mid param\_bit)$

⟨ global variables 11 ⟩ +≡ (195)
 unsigned int *param_mask*, *param_bit*;

Due to forward declarations, procedure calls can occur before the procedure definition. Therefore I can not apply my knowledge about reference parameters when I parse the procedure call, I have to wait for the second pass, when I convert the WEB to cweb. In TEX the procedure identifier (for example *print*) can be a macro, so the procedure identifier is not necessarily preceding the argument list. Hence I have to process the procedure identifier and the argument list separately.

Let's start with the procedure identifier. When I find it, I check for its *value*, and if the value indicates that there is an empty argument list, I add it.

⟨ convert t from WEB to cweb 79 ⟩ +≡ (196)
case PCALLID: DBG($dbgcweb$, "Converting$_\sqcup$call$_\sqcup$in$_\sqcup$line$_\sqcup$%d\n", $t{\rightarrow}lineno$);
 $wid(t)$;
 if (SYM(t)$\rightarrow value \equiv 1$) $wputs("()")$;
 $t = t{\rightarrow}next$; **break**;

At a possibly different place in the WEB file, I will encounter the POPEN token that starts the argument list. It is linked to the corresponding PCLOSE token, and the parser takes care of setting its *up* pointer to the corresponding PCALLID token if there are reference parameters in the argument list.

⟨ convert t from WEB to cweb 79 ⟩ +≡ (197)
case POPEN: $wput('(')$;
 if ($t{\rightarrow}up \equiv \text{NULL} \vee \text{SYM}(t{\rightarrow}up){\rightarrow}value \equiv 0$) $t = wprint\_to(t{\rightarrow}next, t{\rightarrow}link)$;
 else {

```
    int param_mask = SYM(t→up)→value;
    token *close = t→link;
  t = t→next;
  if (param_mask < 0) wput('&');
  param_mask = param_mask ≪ 1;
  while (t ≠ close) {
    if (t→tag ≡ PCOMMA) {
      wputs(",␣"); t = t→next;
      if (param_mask < 0) wput('&');
      param_mask = param_mask ≪ 1;
    }
    else t = wtoken(t);
  }
}
break;
```

5.19 Functions

Functions are slightly more complicated than procedures because they feature a return type and a return value. Let's start with the function header. To find the return type, the parser links the end of the parameter list to the colon and the colon to the end of the return type.

⟨ convert t from WEB to cweb 79 ⟩ +≡   (198)
case PFUNCTION:
```
  {
    token *param = t→link;
    token *type;
    DBG(dbgcweb, "Converting␣function␣heading␣in␣line␣%d\n", t→lineno);
    if (param→tag ≡ POPEN) type = param→link→link;
    else type = param;
    wprint_to(type, type→link); wprint_to(t→next, t→link);
    if (param→tag ≠ POPEN) wputs("(void)");
    else wprint_to(param, param→link→next);
    t = type→link; break;
  }
```

Functions in Pascal return values by assigning them to the function identifier somewhere within the body of the function. In contrast, C uses a return statement, which also terminates the execution of the function immediately. The **return** statement is equivalent to the Pascal assignment only if the assignment is in the tail position of the function. While parsing, I build a tree of the statements. This tree is then searched for assignments to the function identifier in tail positions and these assignments can be converted to **return** statements.

I start with a function that determines whether a part of the parse tree is a "tail", that is it leads directly to the function return.

⟨ functions 13 ⟩ +≡   (199)

5.19 Functions

```
static bool wtail(token *t)
{
  CHECK(t ≠ NULL,
      "Unexpected NULL token while searching for tail statements");
  switch (t→tag) {
  case PSEMICOLON: case PELSE: case CCASE:
    return wtail(t→next) ∧ wtail(t→previous);
  case PCOLON: return wtail(t→next);
  case PRETURN: case CIGNORE: case CEMPTY: return true;
  case PASSIGN: case PCALLID: case PFUNCID: case CRETURN:
    case CPROCRETURN: case PWHILE: case PREPEAT: case PFOR:
    case PEXIT: case PGOTO: return false;
  case PBEGIN: case PIF: case PCASE: return wtail(t→previous);
  default:
    ERROR("Unexpected tag %s while searching for tail statements",
        TAG(t));
  }
}
```

The function *wreturn* accomplishes the main task. It is called by the parser, when it has completed the parsing of the function body with parameter t pointing to the parse tree of the entire body. The parameter *tail*, which tells us if the parse tree t is in a tail position, is then set to true. The link parameter, pointing to a possible PRETURN token, is NULL.

⟨external declarations 5⟩ +≡ (200)
  extern void *wreturn*(**token** *$*t$, **int** *tail*, **token** *$*link$);

The function *wreturn* calls itself recursively to find and convert all instances where a C return statement is appropriate. If I convert the TEX macro "**return**" to a C **return** statement, I decrement its use-count. If at the end it is zero, I can omit the label *end* marking the end of the function body.

⟨functions 13⟩ +≡ (201)
```
  void wreturn(token *t, int tail, token *link)
  {
    CHECK(t ≠ NULL, "Unexpected NULL token while searching f\
        or return statements");
    switch (t→tag) {
    case PSEMICOLON:
      if (t→next→tag ≡ PRETURN) wreturn(t→previous, true, t→next);
      else {
        wreturn(t→next, tail, link);
        if (wtail(t→next)) wreturn(t→previous, tail, link);
        else wreturn(t→previous, false, NULL);
      }
      return;
    case PCOLON: wreturn(t→next, tail, link); return;
```

```
  case PASSIGN: case PCALLID: case PRETURN: case PEXIT: case PGOTO:
  case CIGNORE: case CEMPTY: return;
case PWHILE: case PREPEAT: case PFOR:
    wreturn(t→previous, false, NULL); return;
case PELSE: case CCASE: wreturn(t→next, tail, link);
    wreturn(t→previous, tail, link); return;
case PCASE: case PIF: case PBEGIN: wreturn(t→previous, tail, link);
    return;
case PFUNCID:
    if (tail) {
        DBG(dbgreturn, "Converting assignment to function in line %d\n",
            t→lineno); t→tag = CRETURN; IGN(t→next);
        if (link ≠ NULL) {
            link→sym_ptr→value --; t→sym_ptr = link→sym_ptr;
            IGN(link), IGN(link→next);
            DBG(dbgreturn, "Eliminating label %s (%d) in line %d\n",
                link→sym_ptr→name, link→sym_ptr→value, t→lineno);
        }
    }
    return;
case CRETURN:    /* this happened when the return; is inside a macro */
    if (t→sym_ptr ≠ NULL) {
        t→sym_ptr→value --;
        DBG(dbgreturn, "Eliminating label %s (%d) in line %d\n",
            t→sym_ptr→name, t→sym_ptr→value, t→lineno);
    }
    return;
default: ERROR("Unexpected tag %s in line %d" " while searching fo\
    r return statements", TAG(t), t→lineno);
}
```

After these precautions, there are only two functions left: *x_over_n* in line 2273 and *xn_over_d* in line 2306. These need a special local variable matching the function name in the assignment and a trailing **return** statement.

I have two global variables to hold the symbol numbers of the two function names.

⟨ external declarations 5 ⟩ +≡ (202)
    extern int *x_over_n*, *xn_over_d*;

⟨ global variables 11 ⟩ +≡ (203)
    int *x_over_n*, *xn_over_d*;

⟨ initialize token list 22 ⟩ +≡ (204)
    x_over_n = *get_sym_no*("x_over_n"); *xn_over_d* = *get_sym_no*("xn_over_d");

While parsing, I check for these two function names and change the initial PBEGIN to an PFBEGIN and the trailing PEND to PFEND, setting the *sym_no* of

5.20 The *main* program

these tokens to the symbol number of the function name. Now I can generate the definition of a local variable with the same name as the function (shadowing the function name) at the beginning and a matching return statement at the end.

⟨ convert t from WEB to cweb 79 ⟩ +≡ (205)
case PFBEGIN:
  DBG($dbgcweb$, "Adding␣scaled␣%s;␣in␣line␣%d\n", SYM(t)→$name$, t→$lineno$);
  $wprint$("scaled"); $wid(t)$; $wputs$(";␣"); $t = t$→$next$; **break**;
case PFEND:
  DBG($dbgcweb$, "Adding␣return␣%s;␣in␣line␣%d\n", SYM(t)→$name$, t→$lineno$);
  $wprint$("return"); $wid(t)$; $wputs$(";}"); $t = t$→$next$; **break**;

While converting the token list, I check for PFUNCID and CRETURN tokens

⟨ convert t from WEB to cweb 79 ⟩ +≡ (206)
case PFUNCID:
  DBG($dbgcweb$, "function␣%s␣in␣line␣%d␣assigns␣result␣variable\n",
      SYM(t)→$name$, t→$lineno$); $wid(t)$; $t = t$→$next$; **break**;
case CRETURN:
  DBG($dbgcweb$, "Converted␣function␣return␣%s␣in␣line␣%d\n",
      SYM(t)→$name$, t→$lineno$); $wprint$("return"); $t = t$→$next$; **break**;
case CPROCRETURN:
  if $(t$→sym_ptr→$value \leq 0)$ $wprint$("return");
  else $wprint$("goto␣end");
  $t = t$→$next$; **break**;

5.20 The *main* **program**

While parsing the Pascal program, I change the PBEGIN token starting the main program to a CMAIN token. Now I replace it by the heading of the main program. Similarly I deal with the PEND ending the main program.

⟨ convert t from WEB to cweb 79 ⟩ +≡ (207)
case CMAIN: $wprint$("int␣main(void)␣{"); $t = t$→$next$; **break**;
case CMAINEND: $wprint$("return␣0;␣}"); $t = t$→$next$; **break**;

6 Predefined symbols in Pascal

I put predefine function- and constant-names of Pascal into the symbol table. I omit predefined symbols that are not used in TEX.

⟨initialize token list 22⟩ +≡ (208)
  $predefine($"put"$, \mathrm{PPROCID}, 0);$ $predefine($"get"$, \mathrm{PPROCID}, 0);$
  $predefine($"reset"$, \mathrm{PPROCID}, 0);$ $predefine($"rewrite"$, \mathrm{PPROCID}, 0);$
  $predefine($"abs"$, \mathrm{PFUNCID}, 0);$ $predefine($"odd"$, \mathrm{PFUNCID}, 0);$
  $predefine($"eof"$, \mathrm{PFUNCID}, 0);$ $predefine($"eoln"$, \mathrm{PFUNCID}, 0);$
  $predefine($"round"$, \mathrm{PFUNCID}, 0);$ $predefine($"ord"$, \mathrm{PFUNCID}, 0);$
  $predefine($"chr"$, \mathrm{PFUNCID}, 0);$ $predefine($"close"$, \mathrm{PPROCID}, 0);$
  $predefine($"read"$, \mathrm{PPROCID}, 0);$ $predefine($"read_ln"$, \mathrm{PPROCID}, 0);$
  $predefine($"write"$, \mathrm{PPROCID}, 0);$ $predefine($"write_ln"$, \mathrm{PPROCID}, 0);$
  $predefine($"break"$, \mathrm{PPROCID}, 0);$ $predefine($"break_in"$, \mathrm{PPROCID}, 0);$
  $predefine($"erstat"$, \mathrm{PFUNCID}, 0);$ $predefine($"false"$, \mathrm{PCONSTID}, 0);$
  $predefine($"true"$, \mathrm{PCONSTID}, 1);$

7 Processing the command line

The *usage* function explains command line parameters and options.

⟨ functions 13 ⟩ +≡ (209)
```
void usage(void)
{
  fprintf(stderr,"Usage: web2w [parameters] filename.web\n"
  "Parameters:\n"
  "\t -p   \t generate a pascal output file\n"
  "\t -o file   \t specify an output file name\n"
  "\t -l   \t redirect stderr to a log file\n"
  "\t -y   \t generate a trace while parsing pascal\n"
  "\t -d XX\t hexadecimal debug value. OR together these values:\n"
  "\t \t   \t XX=1    basic debugging\n"
  "\t \t   \t XX=2    flex debugging\n"
  "\t \t   \t XX=4    link debugging\n"
  "\t \t   \t XX=8    token debugging\n"
  "\t \t   \t XX=10  identifier debugging\n"
  "\t \t   \t XX=20  pascal tokens debugging\n"
  "\t \t   \t XX=40  expansion debugging\n"
  "\t \t   \t XX=80  bison debugging\n"
  "\t \t   \t XX=100 pascal parser debugging\n"
  "\t \t   \t XX=200 cweb debugging\n"
  "\t \t   \t XX=400 join debugging\n"
  "\t \t   \t XX=800 string pool debugging\n"
  "\t \t   \t XX=1000 for variables debugging\n"
  "\t \t   \t XX=2000 for real division debugging\n"
  "\t \t   \t XX=4000 for macro debugging\n"
  "\t \t   \t XX=8000 for array debugging\n"
  "\t \t   \t XX=10000 for return debugging\n"
  "\t \t   \t XX=20000 for semicolon debugging\n"
  "\t \t   \t XX=40000 for break debugging\n"
  ); exit(1);
}
```

The different debug values are taken from an enumeration type.

⟨ external declarations 5 ⟩ +≡ (210)
```
typedef enum {
```

$dbgnone = {}^\#0$, $dbgbasic = {}^\#1$, $dbgflex = {}^\#2$, $dbglink = {}^\#4$, $dbgtoken = {}^\#8$,
$dbgid = {}^\#10$, $dbgpascal = {}^\#20$, $dbgexpand = {}^\#40$, $dbgbison = {}^\#80$,
$dbgparse = {}^\#100$, $dbgcweb = {}^\#200$, $dbgjoin = {}^\#400$, $dbgstring = {}^\#800$,
$dbgfor = {}^\#1000$, $dbgslash = {}^\#2000$, $dbgmacro = {}^\#4000$, $dbgarray = {}^\#8000$,
$dbgreturn = {}^\#10000$, $dbgsemicolon = {}^\#20000$, $dbgbreak = {}^\#40000$
} **debugmode**;

Processing the command line looks for options and then sets the basename.

⟨ external declarations 5 ⟩ +≡ (211)
  extern FILE *logfile*;
  extern int *ww_flex_debug*;
  extern debugmode *debugflags*;

⟨ global variables 11 ⟩ +≡ (212)
#**define** MAX_NAME 256
  static char *basename*[MAX_NAME];
  static FILE $*w = \text{NULL}$;
  static FILE $*pascal = \text{NULL}$;
  FILE $*logfile = \text{NULL}$;
  debugmode $debugflags = dbgnone$;

⟨ process the command line 213 ⟩ ≡ (213)
  {
    int $mk\_logfile = 0$, $mk\_pascal = 0$, $baselength = 0$;
    char $*w\_file\_name = \text{NULL}$;

    $ww\_flex\_debug = 0$; $ppdebug = 0$;
    if $(argc < 2)$ $usage(\,)$;
    $argv\mathord{+}\mathord{+}$;   /∗ skip the program name ∗/
    while $(*argv \ne \text{NULL})$ {
      if $((*argv)[0] \equiv \text{'-'})$ {
        char $option = (*argv)[1]$;

        switch $(option)$ {
        default: $usage(\,)$;
        case 'p': $mk\_pascal = 1$; **break**;
        case 'o': $argv\mathord{+}\mathord{+}$; $w\_file\_name = *argv$; **break**;
        case 'l': $mk\_logfile = 1$; **break**;
        case 'y': $ppdebug = 1$; **break**;
        case 'd':
          $argv\mathord{+}\mathord{+}$;
          if $(*argv \equiv \text{NULL})$ $usage(\,)$;
          $debugflags = strtol(*argv, \text{NULL}, 16)$;
          if $(debugflags \mathbin{\&} dbgflex)$ $ww\_flex\_debug = 1$;
          if $(debugflags \mathbin{\&} dbgbison)$ $ppdebug = 1$;
          break;
        }
      }
      else {

7 Processing the command line

$\qquad strncpy(basename, *argv, \mathtt{MAX\_NAME} - 1);$
$\qquad baselength = strlen(basename) - 4;$
$\qquad \textbf{if } (baselength < 1 \lor strncmp(basename + baselength, \mathtt{".web"}, 4) \neq 0)$
$\qquad\qquad usage(\,);$
$\qquad basename[baselength] = 0;$
$\qquad \textbf{if } (*(argv + 1) \neq \mathtt{NULL})\ usage(\,);$
$\quad \}$
$\quad argv\mathbin{++};$
$\}$
⟨ open the files 214 ⟩
$\}$
$\hfill\text{Used in 1.}$

After the command line has been processed, four file streams need to be opened: *win*, the input file; *w*, the output file; *logfile*, if a log file is asked for; and *pascal*, if the output of the pascal code is requested. For technical reasons, the scanner generated by `flex` needs an output file *wwout*. The log file is opened first because this is the place where error messages should go while the other files are opened.

⟨ open the files 214 ⟩ ≡ $\hfill$ (214)
$\quad \textbf{if } (mk\_logfile)\ \{$
$\qquad basename[baselength] = 0;\ strcat(basename, \mathtt{".log"});$
$\qquad logfile = freopen(basename, \mathtt{"w"}, stderr);$
$\qquad \textbf{if } (logfile \equiv \mathtt{NULL})\ \{$
$\qquad\quad fprintf(stderr, \mathtt{"Unable\,to\,open\,logfile\,\%s"}, basename);$
$\qquad\quad logfile = stderr;$
$\qquad \}$
$\qquad wwout = logfile;$
$\quad \}$
$\quad \textbf{else } \{$
$\qquad logfile = stderr;\ wwout = stderr;$
$\quad \}$
$\quad basename[baselength] = 0;\ strcat(basename, \mathtt{".web"});$
$\quad wwin = fopen(basename, \mathtt{"r"});$
$\quad \textbf{if } (wwin \equiv \mathtt{NULL})\ \mathtt{ERROR}(\mathtt{"Unable\,to\,open\,input\,file\,\%s"}, basename);$
$\quad \textbf{if } (w\_file\_name \equiv \mathtt{NULL})\ \{$
$\qquad w\_file\_name = basename;\ basename[baselength] = 0;$
$\qquad strcat(basename, \mathtt{".w"});$
$\quad \}$
$\quad w = fopen(w\_file\_name, \mathtt{"w"});$
$\quad \textbf{if } (w \equiv \mathtt{NULL})\ \mathtt{ERROR}(\mathtt{"Unable\,to\,open\,output\,file\,\%s"}, w\_file\_name);$
$\quad \textbf{if } (mk\_pascal)\ \{$
$\qquad basename[baselength] = 0;\ strcat(basename, \mathtt{".pas"});$
$\qquad pascal = fopen(basename, \mathtt{"w"});$
$\qquad \textbf{if } (pascal \equiv \mathtt{NULL})\ \mathtt{ERROR}(\mathtt{"Unable\,to\,open\,pascal\,file\,\%s"}, basename);$
$\quad \}$
$\hfill\text{Used in 213.}$

8 Error handling and debugging

There is no good program without good error handling. To print messages or indicate errors I define the following macros:

⟨external declarations 5⟩ +≡ (215)
#include <stdlib.h>
#include <stdio.h>
#define MESSAGE(...) (fprintf(logfile, __VA_ARGS__), fflush(logfile))
#define ERROR(...) (fprintf(logfile, "ERROR:␣"), MESSAGE(__VA_ARGS__),
    fprintf(logfile, "\n"), exit(1))
#define CHECK(condition, ...) (¬(condition) ? ERROR(__VA_ARGS__) : 0)

To display the content of a token I can use THE_TOKEN.

⟨external declarations 5⟩ +≡ (216)
#define THE_TOKEN(t) "%d\t%d:␣%s\t[%s]\n", t→lineno, t→sequenceno,
    token2string(t), tagname(t→tag)

The amount of debugging depends on the debugging flags.

⟨external declarations 5⟩ +≡ (217)
#define DBG(flags, ...)
  { if (debugflags & flags) MESSAGE(__VA_ARGS__); }
#define DBGTOKS(flags, from, to)
  {
    if (debugflags & flags) {
      token *t = from;
      MESSAGE("<<");
      while (t ≠ to) {
        MESSAGE("%s", token2string(t)); t = t→next;
      }
      MESSAGE(">>\n");
    }
  }
#define TAG(t) (t ? tagname(t→tag) : "NULL")
#define DBGTREE(flags, t)DBG (flags, "%s␣->␣%s␣|␣%s␣|␣%d\n", TAG(t),
    TAG(t→previous), TAG(t→next), t→value)

9 The scanner

```
%{
#include "web2w.h"
#include "pascal.tab.h"
%}

%option prefix="ww"
%option noyywrap yylineno nounput noinput batch
%option debug

%x PASCAL MIDDLE DEFINITION FORMAT NAME

CONTROL      [^@\n]*
ID           [a-zA-Z][a-zA-Z0-9_]*
SP           [[:blank:]]*
STARSECTION  @\*{SP}(\\\[[0-9a-z]+\])?
SPACESECTION @[[:space:]]{SP}
REAL         [0-9]+(\.[0-9]+(E[+-]?[0-9]+)?|E[+-]?[0-9]+)
DDD          {SP}\.\.\.{SP}
%%
                        /* WEB codes, see WEB User Manual page 7 ff*/
<INITIAL>{
{SPACESECTION}          EOS;TOK("@ ",ATSPACE);BOS;
{STARSECTION}           EOS;TOK("@*",ATSTAR); BOS;
@[dD]                   EOS;TOK("@d ",ATD);BEGIN(DEFINITION);
@[fF]                   EOS;TOK("@f ",ATF);BEGIN(FORMAT);
@[pP]                   EOS;TOK("@p",ATP);PROGRAM;PUSH;SEQ;BEGIN(PASCAL);
@\<{SP}                 EOS;TOK("@<",ATLESS);PUSH;BOS;BEGIN(NAME);

\{                      ADD;PUSH_NULL;
\}                      POP_LEFT;

\|                      EOS;TOK("|",BAR);PUSH;BEGIN(PASCAL);

@'[0-7]+                EOS;TOK(COPY,OCTAL);BOS;
@\"[0-9a-fA-F]+         EOS;TOK(COPY,HEX);BOS;
@\^{CONTROL}@\>         EOS;TOK(COPY,ATINDEX); BOS;
@\.{CONTROL}@\>         EOS;TOK(COPY,ATINDEXTT); BOS;
@\:{CONTROL}@\>         EOS;TOK(COPY,ATINDEX9); BOS;
@!                      EOS;TOK("@!",ATEX); BOS;
```

```
@\?                    EOS;TOK("@?",ATQM); BOS;
@@                     EOS;TOK("@@",ATAT);BOS;
\n                     ADD;
([^\\%@|{}.\n])*       ADD; /* we do not analyze TEX parts any further */
\\[\\%@|{}]            ADD;
\\                     ADD;
\%.*                   ADD;
.                      ADD;
<<EOF>>                EOS;TOK("",WEBEOF);return 0;
}

<MIDDLE>{
{SPACESECTION}         TOK("@ ",ATSPACE);POP;BOS;BEGIN(TEX);
{STARSECTION}          TOK("@*",ATSTAR); POP;BOS;BEGIN(TEX);
@[dD]                  TOK("@d ",ATD);POP;BEGIN(DEFINITION);
@[fF]                  TOK("@f ",ATF);POP;BEGIN(FORMAT);
@[pP]                  TOK("@p",ATP);POP;PROGRAM;PUSH;SEQ;BEGIN(PASCAL);
@\<{SP}                TOK("@<",ATLESS);POP;PUSH;BOS;BEGIN(NAME);
\{                     TOK(" {",MLEFT);PUSH;BEGIN(TEX);BOS;
}

<DEFINITION>{
{ID}                   SYMBOL;
\(#\)                  TOK("(#)",PARAM);
=                      TOK("=",EQEQ);PUSH;DEF_MACRO(NMACRO);BEGIN(MIDDLE);
==                     TOK("==",EQEQ);PUSH;DEF_MACRO(OMACRO);BEGIN(MIDDLE);
[[:space:]]            ;
}

<FORMAT>{
begin                  TOK("if",PIF);
end                    TOK("if",PIF);
{ID}                   SYMBOL;
==                     TOK("==",EQEQ);PUSH;
\{                     TOK(" {",MLEFT);PUSH;BEGIN(TEX);BOS;
\n                     TOK("\n",NL);BEGIN(MIDDLE);
[[:space:]]            ;
}

<NAME>{
{SP}@\>                EOS;AT_GREATER;BEGIN(PASCAL);
{DDD}@\>               EOS;TOK("...",ELIPSIS);AT_GREATER;BEGIN(PASCAL);
{SP}@\>{SP}=           EOS;AT_GREATER_EQ;BEGIN(PASCAL);
{DDD}@\>{SP}=          EOS;TOK("...",ELIPSIS);AT_GREATER_EQ;BEGIN(PASCAL);
[[:space:]]+           add_string(" ");
.                      ADD;
}
```

9 The scanner

```
<PASCAL>{
{SPACESECTION}         TOK("@ ",ATSPACE);POP;BOS;BEGIN(TEX);
{STARSECTION}          TOK("@*",ATSTAR);POP;BOS;BEGIN(TEX);
@\<{SP}                TOK("@<",ATLESS);PUSH;BOS;BEGIN(NAME);
\{                     TOK(" {",PLEFT);PUSH;BEGIN(TEX);BOS;
}

<MIDDLE,PASCAL>{
<<EOF>>                TOK("",WEBEOF);POP;return 0;

@'[0-7]+               TOK(COPY,OCTAL);
@\"[0-9a-fA-F]+        TOK(COPY,HEX);
@!                     TOK("@!",ATEX);
@\?                    TOK("@?",ATQM);
\|                     TOK("|",BAR);POP;BEGIN(TEX);BOS;
@t{CONTROL}@\>         TOK(COPY,ATT);
@={CONTROL}@\>         TOK(COPY,ATEQ);

\}                     ERROR("Unexpected }");
\(                     TOK("(",POPEN);PUSH;
\)                     TOK(")",PCLOSE);POP;
#                      TOK("#",HASH);/* used in macros */

                       /* non Pascal tokens */
\n                     TOK("\n",NL);
@\^{CONTROL}@\>        TOK(COPY,ATINDEX);
@\.{CONTROL}@\>        TOK(COPY,ATINDEXTT);
@\:{CONTROL}@\>        TOK(COPY,ATINDEX9);
@\$                    TOK("@$",ATDOLLAR);
@\{                    TOK("@{",ATLEFT);
@\}                    TOK("@}",ATRIGHT);
@\{[^\n]*@\}           TOK(COPY,METACOMMENT);
@\&                    TOK("@&",ATAND);
@\\                    TOK("@\\",ATBACKSLASH);
@,                     TOK("@,",ATCOMMA);
@\/                    TOK("@/",ATSLASH);
@\|                    TOK("@|",ATBAR);
@\#                    TOK("@#",ATHASH);
@\+                    TOK("@+",ATPLUS);
@\;                    TOK("@;",ATSEMICOLON);

                       /* Pascal tokens */
=                      TOK("=",PEQ);
\+                     TOK("+",PPLUS);
\-                     TOK("-",PMINUS);
\*                     TOK("*",PSTAR);
\/                     TOK("/",PSLASH);
\<\>                   TOK(" <> ",PNOTEQ);
\<                     TOK(" < ",PLESS);
```

```
\>                    TOK(" > ",PGREATER);
\<=                   TOK(" <= ",PLESSEQ);
\>=                   TOK(" >= ",PGREATEREQ);
\[                    TOK("[",PSQOPEN);
\]                    TOK("]",PSQCLOSE);
:=                    TOK(":=",PASSIGN);
\.                    TOK(".",PDOT);
\.\.                  TOK("..",PDOTDOT);
,                     TOK(",",PCOMMA);
;                     TOK(";",PSEMICOLON);
:                     TOK(": ",PCOLON);
\^                    TOK("^",PUP);

                      /* special coding trick in line 676 of tex.web */
t@&y@&p@&e            TOK("type",PTYPE);

                      /* pascal keywords */
"mod"                 TOK("mod",PMOD);
"div"                 TOK("div",PDIV);
"nil"                 TOK("nil",PNIL);
"in"                  TOK("in",PIN);
"or"                  TOK("or",POR);
"and"                 TOK("and",PAND);
"not"                 TOK("not",PNOT);
"if"                  TOK("if",PIF);
"then"                TOK("then",PTHEN);
"else"                TOK("else",PELSE);
"case"                TOK("case",PCASE);
"of"                  TOK("of",POF);
"others"              TOK("others",POTHERS);
"forward"             TOK("forward",PFORWARD);
"repeat"              TOK("repeat",PREPEAT);
"until"               TOK("until",PUNTIL);
"while"               TOK("while",PWHILE);
"do"                  TOK("do",PDO);
"for"                 TOK("for",PFOR);
"to"                  TOK("to",PTO);
"downto"              TOK("downto",PDOWNTO);
"begin"               TOK("begin",PBEGIN);
"end"                 TOK("end",PEND);
"with"                TOK("with",PWITH);
"goto"                TOK("goto",PGOTO);
"const"               TOK("const",PCONST);
"var"                 TOK("var",PVAR);
"array"               TOK("array",PARRAY);
"record"              TOK("record",PRECORD);
"set"                 TOK("set",PSET);
```

9 The scanner

```
"file"                  TOK("file",PFILE);
"function"              TOK("function",PFUNCTION);
"procedure"             TOK("procedure",PPROCEDURE);
"label"                 TOK("label",PLABEL);
"packed"                TOK("packed",PPACKED);
"program"               TOK("program",PPROGRAM);
"char"                  TOK("char",PTYPECHAR);
"integer"               TOK("integer",PTYPEINT);
"real"                  TOK("real",PTYPEREAL);
"boolean"               TOK("boolean",PTYPEBOOL);

"endcases"              TOK("endcases",PEND);
"othercases"            TOK("othercases",POTHERS);
"mtype"                 TOK("type",PTYPE);
"final_end"             TOK("final_end",PEXIT);

"return"                TOK_RETURN;

"debug"                 TOK("debug",WDEBUG);
"gubed"                 TOK("debug",WGUBED);
"stat"                  TOK("stat",WSTAT);
"tats"                  TOK("tats",WTATS);
"init"                  TOK("init",WINIT);
"tini"                  TOK("tini",WTINI);

{ID}                    SYMBOL;
\"([^"\n]|\"\")\"       TOK(COPY,CHAR);    /* single character string */
\"([^"\n]|\"\")*\"      WWSTRING; /* multiple character string */
\'([^'\n]|\'\'|@@)\'    TOK(COPY,PCHAR);
\'([^'\n]|\'\')*\'      TOK(COPY,PSTRING);
[0-9]+                  TOK(COPY,PINTEGER);
{REAL}                  TOK(COPY,PREAL);

^[[:space:]]+           TOK(COPY,INDENT);
[[:space:]]             ; /* in Pascal mode we ignore spaces */

}

                        /* anything that gets to this line
                           is an illegal character */
<*>.                    { ERROR("Illegal %c (0x%02x) in line %d mode %d",
                          yytext[0],yytext[0],yylineno, YY_START);}

%%
```

10 The parser

The following code is contained in the file pascal.y. It represents a modified grammar for the Pascal language. Here and throughout of this document, terminal symbols, or tokens, are shown using a small caps font; for nonterminal symbols I use a slanted font.

```
%{
#include <stdio.h>
#include "web2w.h"

/* the tag=token number of the left hand side symbol of a rule */
#define LHSS (yyr1[yyn]+FIRST_PASCAL_TOKEN-3)

static int function=0;

%}
%code requires {
#define PPSTYPE token *
#define YYSTYPE PPSTYPE

extern int ppparse(void);
extern int ppdebug;
}
%token-table
%defines
%error_verbose
%debug
%define api.prefix "pp"
%expect 1

%token PEOF 0 "end of file"
%token WEBEOF "end of web"
%token HEAD
%token BAR
%token PLEFT
%token MLEFT
%token RIGHT
%token OPEN
%token CLOSE
```

```
%token TEXT
%token NL
%token HASH
%token NMACRO
%token OMACRO
%token PMACRO
%token PARAM
%token EQ
%token EQEQ
%token ATSTAR
%token ATSPACE
%token ATD
%token ATF
%token ATLESS
%token ATGREATER
%token ELIPSIS
%token ATP
%token OCTAL
%token HEX
%token ATAT
%token ATDOLLAR
%token ATLEFT
%token ATRIGHT
%token ATINDEX
%token ATINDEXTT
%token ATINDEX9
%token ATT
%token ATEQ
%token ATAND
%token ATBACKSLASH
%token ATEX
%token ATQM
%token ATCOMMA
%token ATSLASH
%token ATBAR
%token ATHASH
%token ATPLUS
%token ATSEMICOLON
%token STRING
%token CHAR
%token INDENT
%token METACOMMENT
%token CSEMICOLON
%token ID

%token WDEBUG
```

10 The parser

```
%token WSTAT
%token WINIT
%token WTINI
%token WTATS
%token WGUBED

%token PRETURN "return"

%token FIRST_PASCAL_TOKEN

%token PPLUS "+"
%token PMINUS "-"
%token PSTAR "*"
%token PSLASH "/"
%token PEQ "="
%token PNOTEQ "<>"
%token PLESS "<"
%token PGREATER ">"
%token PLESSEQ "<="
%token PGREATEREQ ">="
%token POPEN "("
%token PCLOSE ")"
%token PSQOPEN "["
%token PSQCLOSE "]"
%token PASSIGN ":="
%token PDOT "."
%token PCOMMA ","
%token PSEMICOLON ";"
%token PMOD "mod"
%token PDIV "div"
%token PNIL "nil"
%token POR "or"
%token PAND "and"
%token PNOT "not"
%token PIF "if"
%token PTHEN "then"
%token PELSE "else"
%token PREPEAT "repeat"
%token PUNTIL "until"
%token PWHILE "while"
%token PDO "do"
%token PFOR "for"
%token PTO "to"
%token PDOWNTO "downto"
%token PBEGIN "begin"
%token PEND "end"
%token PGOTO "goto"
```

```
%token PINTEGER "0-9"
%token PREAL "real"
%token POTHERS "others"
%token PSTRING "'...'"
%token PCHAR "'.'"
%token PTYPECHAR "char type"
%token PTYPEBOOL "bool type"
%token PTYPEINT "integer type"
%token PTYPEREAL "real type"
%token PTYPEINDEX "index type"

%token PID "identifier"
%token PDEFVARID "variable definition"
%token PDEFPARAMID "parameter definition"
%token PDEFREFID "reference parameter definition"
%token PCONSTID "constant"
%token PDEFCONSTID "constant definition"
%token PDEFTYPEID "typename definition"
%token PDEFTYPESUBID "subrange typename definition"
%token PARRAYFILETYPEID "array of file type"
%token PARRAYFILEID "array of file name"
%token PFUNCID "functionname"
%token PDEFFUNCID "functionname definition"
%token PPROCID "procedurename"
%token PCALLID "call"
%token PRETURNID "return value"

%token PEXIT "final_end"
%token PFBEGIN "function begin"
%token PFEND "function end"
%token PDOTDOT ".."
%token PCOLON ":"
%token PUP "^"
%token PIN "in"
%token PCASE "case"
%token POF "of"
%token PWITH "with"
%token PCONST "const"
%token PVAR "var"
%token PTYPE "type"
%token PARRAY "array"
%token PRECORD "record"
%token PSET "set"
%token PFILE "file"
%token PFUNCTION "function"
%token PPROCEDURE "procedure"
%token PLABEL "label"
```

10 The parser

```
%token PPACKED "packed"
%token PPROGRAM "program"
%token PFORWARD "forward"

%token CIGNORE
%token CLABEL
%token CLABELN
%token CINTDEF
%token CSTRDEF
%token CMAIN
%token CMAINEND
%token CUNION
%token CTSUBRANGE
%token CINT
%token CREFID "reference variable"
%token CRETURN "C function return"
%token CPROCRETURN "C procedure return"
%token CCASE "C case"
%token CCOLON "C :"
%token CBREAK "break"
%token CEMPTY "empty statement"
%%
```

program : *programheading globals*
        PBEGIN *statements* PEND PDOT
        { CHGTAG($3,CMAIN); CHGTAG($5,CMAINEND); IGN($6);
          wsemicolon($4,$5);
        }
    ;

programheading : PPROGRAM PID PSEMICOLON { IGN($2); IGN($3); }
    ;

globals : *labels constants types variables procedures*
    ;

labels :
    | PLABEL *labellist* PSEMICOLON { IGN($3); }
    ;

labellist : *labeldecl*
    | *labellist* PCOMMA *labeldecl* { IGN($2); }
    ;

labeldecl : NMACRO { IGN($1); SYM($1)->obsolete=1; }
    | PINTEGER { IGN($1); }
    | PEXIT { IGN($1); }
    | *labeldecl* PPLUS PINTEGER { IGN($2); IGN($3); }
    ;

constants :
          | PCONST *constdefinitions*
          | PCONST *constdefinitions conststringdefinition*
          ;

constdefinitions : *constdefinition*
            | *constdefinitions constdefinition*
            ;

constdefinition : PID PEQ PINTEGER PSEMICOLON { LNK($1,$2); LNK($2,$4);
         SETVAL($1,getval($3)); CHGID($1,PCONSTID);
         CHGTAG($1,CINTDEF); }
         ;

conststringdefinition : PID PEQ PSTRING PSEMICOLON
            { seq($1,$4); CHGID($1,PCONSTID);
           CHGTAG($1,CSTRDEF);CHGTAG($2,PASSIGN); }
          ;

types :
      | PTYPE *typedefinitions* { IGN($1); }
      ;

typedefinitions : *typedefinition*
          | *typedefinitions typedefinition*
          ;

typedefinition : PID PEQ *subrange* PSEMICOLON
        { DBG(dbgparse,"New Subrange Type: %s\n",
        SYM($1)->name);
        LNK($1,$2); IGN($2);LNK($2,$4);
        CHGTYPE($1,$3);
        CHGTAG($1,PDEFTYPEID);
        CHGTAG($2,CTSUBRANGE); UP($2,$3);
        }
       | PID PEQ *type* PSEMICOLON
        { DBG(dbgparse,"New Type: %s\n",
        SYM($1)->name);
        LNK($1,$2); IGN($2); LNK($2,$4);
        CHGTYPE($1,$3); LNK($3,$4);
        CHGTAG($1,PDEFTYPEID);
        }
        ;

10 The parser

subrange : *iconst* PDOTDOT *iconst*
    { $$=join(PDOTDOT,$1,$3,$3->value-$1->value+1); }
    | PTYPECHAR
    { $$=join(PDOTDOT,join(PTYPECHAR,$1,$1,0),
      join(PTYPECHAR,$1,$1,255),256); }
    ;

iconst : *signed_iconst* { $$=$1; }
    | *iconst* PPLUS *simple_iconst*
    { $$=join(PPLUS,$1,$3,$1->value+$3->value); }
    | *iconst* PMINUS *simple_iconst*
    { $$=join(PMINUS,$1,$3,$1->value-$3->value); }
    ;

signed_iconst : *simple_iconst* { $$=$1; }
    | PPLUS *simple_iconst* { $$=join(PPLUS,NULL,$2,$2->value); }
    | PMINUS *simple_iconst*
     { $$=join(PMINUS,NULL,$2,-($2->value)); }
    ;

simple_iconst : PINTEGER { $$=join(PINTEGER,$1,NULL,getval($1)); }
    | NMACRO { $$=join(NMACRO,$1,NULL,getval($1)); }
    | PCONSTID { $$=join(PCONSTID,$1,NULL,getval($1)); }
    ;

file_type : *packed* PFILE POF *typename* { $$=$2; }
    | *packed* PFILE POF *subrange* { $$=$2; }
    ;

packed : PPACKED
    |
    ;

typename : PTYPEINT { $$=NULL; }
    | PTYPEREAL { $$=NULL; }
    | PTYPEBOOL { $$=NULL; }
    | PID { $$=NULL; }
    ;

record_type : *packed* PRECORD *fields* PEND { LNK($2,$4); LNK($3,$4);
      if ($3) CHGTAG($4,PSEMICOLON); else IGN($4); $$=NULL; }
    | *packed* PRECORD *variant_part* PEND
    { LNK($2,$4); LNK($3,$4); IGN($4); $$=NULL; }
    | *packed* PRECORD *fields* PSEMICOLON *variant_part* PEND
    { LNK($2,$6); LNK($3,$4); LNK($5,$6); IGN($6); $$=NULL; }
    ;

fields : *recordsection* { $$=$1; }
    | *fields* PSEMICOLON *recordsection* { LNK($1,$2); $$=$3; }
    ;

/* in a recordsection the first PID links to the PCOLON, the recordsection
   points to the PCOLON   */
recordsection : { $$=NULL; }
            | *recids* PCOLON *type* { LNK($1,$2); IGN($2); $$=$2; }
            | *recids* PCOLON *subrange*
              { LNK($1,$2); CHGTAG($2,CTSUBRANGE); UP($2,$3); $$=$2; }
            ;

/* recids point to the first PID which is changed to PDEFVARID   */
recids : PID { $$=$1; CHGTAG($1,PDEFVARID); }
       | *recids* PCOMMA PID { $$=$1; }
       ;

variant_part : PCASE PID POF *variants* { IGN($1);IGN($2);
              CHGTAG($3,CUNION); $$=$3; }
           ;

variants : *variant*
         | *variants variant*
         ;

variant : PINTEGER PCOLON POPEN *recordsection* PCLOSE PSEMICOLON
        { IGN($1); IGN($2); IGN($3);
          LNK($4,$5);
          IGN($5); }
      | PINTEGER PCOLON POPEN *recordsection* PSEMICOLON
        recordsection PCLOSE PSEMICOLON
        { IGN($1); IGN($2); CHGTAG($3,PRECORD);
          LNK($3,$8); LNK($4,$5); LNK($6,$7); CHGTAG($7,PSEMICOLON); }
      ;

type : *typename*
     | *file_type*
     | *record_type*
     ;

10 The parser

array_type : *packed* PARRAY PSQOPEN *iconst* PDOTDOT *iconst* PSQCLOSE
POF *type* { LNK($2,$3);
UP($2,join(PDOTDOT,$4,$6,$6->value-$4->value+1));
LNK($3,$5); LNK($5,$7); LNK($7,$8);$$=$8; }
| *packed* PARRAY PSQOPEN *iconst* PDOTDOT *iconst* PSQCLOSE
POF *subrange* { LNK($2,$3);
UP($2,join(PDOTDOT,$4,$6,$6->value-$4->value+1));
LNK($3,$5); LNK($5,$7); LNK($7,$8);
CHGTAG($8,CTSUBRANGE); UP($8,$9);$$=$8; }
| *packed* PARRAY PSQOPEN PID PSQCLOSE POF *type* { LNK($2,$3);
UP($2,$4);LNK($3,$4); LNK($4,$5); LNK($5,$6);$$=$6; }
| *packed* PARRAY PSQOPEN PID PSQCLOSE POF *subrange*
{ LNK($2,$3); UP($2,$4); LNK($3,$4); LNK($4,$5);
LNK($5,$6); CHGTAG($6,CTSUBRANGE); UP($6,$7);$$=$6; }
| *packed* PARRAY PSQOPEN PTYPECHAR PSQCLOSE
POF *type* { LNK($2,$3); UP($2,join(PDOTDOT,
join(PTYPECHAR,$1,$1,0),join(PTYPECHAR,$1,$1,255),256));
$3->link=join(PTYPECHAR,$3,$5,256); $3->link->link=$5;
/* the PTYPECHAR comes from a macroexpansion, so we can not
link it directly */ LNK($5,$6); $$=$6; }
;

variables :
| PVAR *vardeclarations* { IGN($1); }
;

vardeclarations : *vardeclaration*
| *vardeclarations vardeclaration*
;

vardeclaration : *varids* PCOLON *type* PSEMICOLON { LNK($1,$2);
IGN($2); LNK($2,$4); }
| *varids* PCOLON *array_type* PSEMICOLON { LNK($1,$2);
IGN($2); LNK($3,$4); LNK($2,$4); }
| *varids* PCOLON *subrange* PSEMICOLON { LNK($1,$2);
CHGTAG($2,CTSUBRANGE); UP($2,$3); LNK($2,$4); }
;

varids : *entire_var* { CHGTAG($1,PDEFVARID); $$=$1; }
| *varids* PCOMMA *entire_var* { LNK($1,$3);$$=$3; }
;

procedures :
| *procedures procedure*
| *procedures function*
;

locals : PVAR *localvardeclarations* { CHGTAG($1,PBEGIN); }
　　　| PLABEL *locallabellist* PSEMICOLON *localvariables*
　　　　{ CHGTAG($1,PBEGIN); IGN($3); }
　　　;

locallabellist : *locallabeldecl*
　　　　　| *locallabellist* PCOMMA *locallabeldecl* { IGN($2); }
　　　　　;

locallabeldecl : NMACRO { IGN($1); SYM($1)->obsolete=1; localize($1); }
　　　　　| PINTEGER { IGN($1); }
　　　　　| *labeldecl* PPLUS PINTEGER { IGN($2); IGN($3); }
　　　　　;

localvariables :
　　　　　| PVAR *localvardeclarations* { IGN($1); }
　　　　　;

localvardeclarations : *localvardeclaration*
　　　　　　　　| *localvardeclarations* *localvardeclaration*
　　　　　　　　;

localvardeclaration : *localvarids* PCOLON *type* PSEMICOLON
　　　　　　　{ LNK($1,$2); IGN($2); LNK($2,$4); }
　　　　　　| *localvarids* PCOLON *array_type* PSEMICOLON
　　　　　　　{ LNK($1,$2); IGN($2); LNK($3,$4); LNK($2,$4); }
　　　　　　| *localvarids* PCOLON *subrange* PSEMICOLON
　　　　　　　{ LNK($1,$2); CHGTAG($2,CTSUBRANGE);
　　　　　　　　UP($2,$3); LNK($2,$4); }
　　　　　　;

localvarids : *localentire_var* { CHGTAG($1,PDEFVARID); $$=$1; }
　　　　　| *localvarids* PCOMMA *localentire_var* { LNK($1,$3);$$=$3; }
　　　　　;

localentire_var : PID { $$=$1; localize($1); }
　　　　　　| CREFID { $$=$1; CHGTAG($1,PID);
　　　　　　　　CHGID($1,PID); localize($1); }
　　　　　　;

procedure : *pheading locals* PBEGIN *statements* PEND PSEMICOLON
　　　　　{ IGN($3); IGN($6); wend($4,$5); wsemicolon($4,$5);
　　　　　　scope_close(); }
　　　　| *pheading* PBEGIN *statements* PEND PSEMICOLON
　　　　　{ IGN($5); wend($3,$4); wsemicolon($3,$4); scope_close(); }
　　　　| *pheading* PFORWARD PSEMICOLON { scope_close(); }
　　　　;

10 The parser

```
function : fheading PBEGIN { function=1; }statements PEND PSEMICOLON
            { function=0; wreturn($4, 1,NULL); IGN($6);
              wsemicolon($4,$5); scope_close(); }
         | fheading locals PBEGIN { function=1; }
           statements PEND PSEMICOLON
           { int f_no=$1->sym_no;
             function=0;
             if (f_no==x_over_n || f_no==xn_over_d)
             { DBG(dbgcweb,"Discovered function %s; in line %d\n",
               SYM($1)->name,$1->lineno);
               CHGTAG($3,PFBEGIN); $3->sym_no=f_no;
               CHGTAG($6,PFEND); $6->sym_no=f_no;
             }
             else
             { IGN($3);
               wreturn($5,1,NULL);
             }
             wsemicolon($5,$6);
             IGN($7);
             scope_close();
           }
         ;
pid : PID { scope_open(); $$=$1; START_PARAM; }
    | PPROCID { scope_open(); $$=$1; START_PARAM; }
    | PFUNCID { scope_open(); $$=$1; START_PARAM; }
    ;

pheading : PPROCEDURE pid PSEMICOLON
           { LNK($1,$3); CHGID($2,PPROCID); CHGVALUE($2,1); IGN($3); }
         | PPROCEDURE pid POPEN formals PCLOSE PSEMICOLON
           { LNK($1,$3); CHGID($2,PPROCID); CHGVALUE($2,param_mask);
             LNK($4,$5); IGN($6); }
         ;

fheading : PFUNCTION pid PCOLON typename PSEMICOLON
           { $$=$2; LNK($1,$3); CHGID($2,PFUNCID);
             CHGVALUE($2,1);IGN($3); LNK($3,$5); IGN($5); }
         | PFUNCTION pid POPEN formals PCLOSE
           PCOLON typename PSEMICOLON { $$=$2; LNK($1,$3);
             CHGID($2,PFUNCID); CHGVALUE($2,param_mask);
             LNK($4,$5); LNK($5,$6); IGN($6); LNK($6,$8); IGN($8); }
         ;
```

formals : *formalparameters* { $$=$1; }
   | *formals* PSEMICOLON *formalparameters*
      { LNK($1,$2); CHGTAG($2,PCOMMA); $$=$3; }
   ;

formalparameters : *params* PCOLON *typename*
            { LNK($1,$2); IGN($2); $$=$2; }
         ;

params : *param* { $$=$1; }
   | *params* PCOMMA *param* { LNK($1,$3);$$=$3; }
   ;

param : *entire_var* { NEXT_PARAM; CHGTAG($1,PDEFPARAMID); $$=$1; }
   | PVAR *entire_var* { REF_PARAM; NEXT_PARAM; IGN($1);
      CHGTAG($2,PDEFREFID);CHGID($2,CREFID); $$=$2; }
   ;

proc_stmt : PPROCID POPEN *args* PCLOSE { CHGTAG($1,PCALLID); $$=$1;
         UP($2,$1); pstring_args($1,$3); }
      | PCALLID POPEN *args* PCLOSE
         { $$=$1; UP($2,$1); pstring_args($1,$3); }
      | PPROCID { CHGTAG($1,PCALLID); $$=$1; }
      | PCALLID { $$=$1; }
      ;

function_call : PFUNCID POPEN *args* PCLOSE
            { CHGTAG($1,PCALLID); $$=$4; UP($2,$1); }
         | PCALLID POPEN *args* PCLOSE { $$=$4; UP($2,$1); }
         | PFUNCID { CHGTAG($1,PCALLID);$$=$1; }
         | PCALLID { $$=$1; }
         ;

args : *arg* { $$=$1; }
   | *args* PCOMMA *arg*
      { if ($3==NULL) $$=$1; else if ($1==NULL) $$=$3;
        else $$=join(PCOMMA,$1,$3,0); }
   ;

arg : *expression* { $$=$1; }
   | *write_arg* { $$=$1; }
   | STRING { $$=$1; }
   | CHAR { $$=$1; }
   ;

write_arg : *expression* PCOLON *expression* { $$=$2; }
      ;

10 The parser

```
statements : statement { $$=$1; }
           | statements PSEMICOLON statement
             { $$=join(PSEMICOLON,$1,$3,0); }
           ;

statement : stmt { $$=$1; }
          | label PCOLON stmt { clabel($1,0);$$=join(PCOLON,$1,$3,0); }
          | PEXIT PCOLON stmt
            { IGN($1); IGN($2); $$=join(PCOLON,$1,$3,0); }
          ;

goto_stmt : PGOTO label { clabel($2,1); $$=join(PGOTO,$2,NULL,0); }
          | PGOTO PEXIT { IGN($1); $$=$2; }
          | CIGNORE PEXIT { $$=$2; }
          | PRETURN { if (function) clabel($1,1);
              else { CHGTAG($1,CPROCRETURN);$1->sym_ptr->value++; }
              $$=$1; }
          ;

label : PINTEGER
      | NMACRO
      | CLABEL
      | NMACRO PPLUS PINTEGER { seq($1,$3); $$=$1; }
      ;

stmt : simple_stmt
     | structured_stmt
     ;

simple_stmt : empty_stmt
            | assign_stmt
            | return_stmt
            | goto_stmt
            | proc_stmt
            ;

empty_stmt : { $$=join(CEMPTY,NULL,NULL,0); }
           ;

assign_stmt : variable PASSIGN expression { $$=$2; }
            | variable PASSIGN STRING { $$=$2; pstring_assign($1,$3); }
            | variable PASSIGN POPEN STRING PCLOSE
              { $$=$2; pstring_assign($1,$4); }
            ;
```

return_stmt : PFUNCID PASSIGN *expression* { $$=$1; }
          | CRETURN CIGNORE *expression* { $$=$1; }
          | CRETURN CIGNORE *expression* CIGNORE CIGNORE
            { $$=join(CRETURN,NULL,NULL,0); }
          | CRETURN { $$=$1; }
          | CPROCRETURN { $$=$1; }
          ;

structured_stmt : *compound_stmt*
               | *conditional_stmt*
               | *repetitive_stmt*
               ;

compound_stmt : PBEGIN *statements* PEND
              { $$=join(PBEGIN,$2,NULL,0); wsemicolon($2,$3); }
          ;

conditional_stmt : *if_stmt*
                | *case_stmt*
                ;

if_stmt : PIF *expression* PTHEN *statement* { $$=join(PIF,$4,NULL,0); }
       | PIF *expression* PTHEN *statement* PELSE *statement*
         { wsemicolon($4,$5); $$=join(PELSE,$4,$6,0); }
       ;

case_stmt : PCASE *expression* POF *case_list* PEND { LNK($1,$3);
             wsemicolon($4,$5);$$=join(PCASE,$4,NULL,0); }
         | PCASE *expression* POF *case_list* PSEMICOLON PEND
           { LNK($1,$3);$$=join(PCASE,$4,NULL,0); }
         ;

case_list : *case_element*
          | *case_list* PSEMICOLON *case_element* { $$=join(CCASE,$1,$3,0);
            wsemicolon($1,$2); CHGTAG($2,CBREAK); UP($2,$1); }
          | *case_list* CBREAK *case_element*
            { $$=join(CCASE,$1,$3,0); /* etex parses same module twice */ }
          ;

case_element : *case_labels* PCOLON *statement* { $$=$3; }
            | POTHERS *statement* { $$=$2; }
            ;

case_labels : *case_label*
             | *case_labels* PCOMMA *case_label*
               { CHGTAG($2,CCOLON); CHGTEXT($2,": "); }
             | *case_labels* CCOLON *case_label*
             ;

10 The parser

```
case_label : PINTEGER { winsert_after($1->previous,CCASE,"case "); }
           | NMACRO { winsert_after($1->previous,CCASE,"case "); }
           | PINTEGER PPLUS NMACRO
             { winsert_after($1->previous,CCASE,"case "); }
           | NMACRO PPLUS NMACRO
             { winsert_after($1->previous,CCASE,"case "); }
           | NMACRO PPLUS PINTEGER
             { winsert_after($1->previous,CCASE,"case "); }
           | CCASE NMACRO
           | CCASE PINTEGER
           | CCASE NMACRO PPLUS NMACRO
           | NMACRO PMINUS NMACRO PPLUS NMACRO
             { winsert_after($1->previous,CCASE,"case "); /* etex */ }
           ;

repetitive_stmt : while_stmt
                | repeat_stmt
                | for_stmt
                ;

while_stmt : PWHILE expression PDO statement
             { LNK($1,$3); $$=join(PWHILE,$4,NULL,0); }
           ;

repeat_stmt : PREPEAT statements PUNTIL expression
              { wsemicolon($2,$3); $$=join(PREPEAT,$2,NULL,0); }
            ;

for_stmt : PFOR PID PASSIGN expression PTO varlimit PDO statement
           { mark_for_variable($2,$1->lineno,0,VAR_LOOP);
             DBG(dbgfor,"for variable %s, limit variable in line %d\n",
             SYM($2)->name,$2->lineno);
             $$=join(PFOR,$8,NULL,0);LNK($1,$5);LNK($5,$7); }
         | PFOR PID PASSIGN expression PTO iconst PDO statement
           { mark_for_variable($2,$1->lineno,$6->value,TO_LOOP);
             DBG(dbgfor,"for variable %s, limit up in line %d\n",
             SYM($2)->name,$2->lineno);
             $$=join(PFOR,$8,NULL,0);LNK($1,$5);LNK($5,$7); }
         | PFOR PID PASSIGN expression PDOWNTO iconst PDO statement
           { mark_for_variable($2,$1->lineno,$6->value,DOWNTO_LOOP);
             DBG(dbgfor,"for variable %s, limit down in line %d\n",
             SYM($2)->name,$2->lineno);
             $$=join(PFOR,$8,NULL,0);LNK($1,$5);LNK($5,$7); }
         ;
```

varlimit : *variable*
       | *variable* PMINUS *expression*
       | *variable* PPLUS *expression*
       | *iconst* PSTAR *expression*
       ;

variable : PID
       | CREFID
       | *indexed_var*
       | *field_var*
       | *file_var*
       ;

entire_var : PID { $$=$1; }
       | CREFID { $$=$1; CHGTAG($1,PID); CHGID($1,PID); }
       ;

indexed_var : *variable* PSQOPEN *expression* PSQCLOSE
       | *variable* PSQOPEN STRING PSQCLOSE
       | PARRAYFILEID PSQOPEN *expression* PSQCLOSE
       ;

field_var : *variable* PDOT PID
       ;

file_var : *variable* PUP
       ;

expression : *simple_expr* { $$=$1; }
       | *simple_expr* *relop* *simple_expr* { $$=$3; }
       | *simple_expr* PEQ STRING { $$=$3; }
       ;

relop : PEQ
     | PNOTEQ
     | PLESS
     | PLESSEQ
     | PGREATER
     | PGREATEREQ
     ;

simple_expr : *term* { $$=$1; }
       | *sign* *term* { $$=$2; }
       | *simple_expr* *addop* *term* { $$=$3; }
       | *simple_expr* *addop* *sign* *term* { $$=$4; }
       ;

sign : PPLUS
   | PMINUS
   ;

10 The parser

```
addop : PPLUS
      | PMINUS
      | POR
      ;

term : factor { $$=$1; }
     | term mulop factor { $$=$3; }
     ;

mulop : PSTAR
      | PSLASH { DBG(dbgslash,"Pascal / in line %d\n",$1->lineno); }
      | PDIV
      | PMOD
      | PAND
      ;

factor : variable
       | unsigned_const
       | POPEN expression PCLOSE { $$=$3; }
       | function_call
       | PNOT factor { $$=$2; }
       ;

unsigned_const : real
               | PINTEGER
               | NMACRO
               | PSTRING
               | PCHAR
               | PCONSTID
               ;

real : PREAL
     | PINTEGER PDOT PINTEGER { $$=$3; /* used in line 2361 */}
     ;

%%

const char *tagname(int tag)
{ return yytname[YYTRANSLATE(tag)];
}
```

11 Generating TeX, Running TeX, and Passing the Trip Test

Here I give a step by step instruction on how to get TeX up and running and finally, how to pass Donald Knuth's trip test.

I assume that you have a Unix/Linux system with a terminal window but other operating systems might work as well as long as you have access to the internet (I need files from www.ctan.org), an unzip program (because packages on www.ctan.org come in .zip files), and a C compiler.

The recommended, short, and easy way is to start with the file ctex.w the cweb version of tex.web. After all, this is the reason for the whole web2w project: to provide you with a cweb version of TeX that is much easier to use than the original WEB version of TeX. But if you insist, there is also a subsection below that explains how to get web2w up and running and use it to generate the ctex.w file.

11.1 Generating TeX

1. Download the web2w package from www.ctan.org and expand the files. Open a terminal window and navigate to the root directory of the package. This directory will be called the web2w directory in the following. It contains a Makefile that contains most of the commands that are explained in the following.

2. In the web2w directory are the files ctex.c and ctex.tex. If you want to use them, go to step 7; if you want to build them yourself, continue with the next step.

3. TeX and web2w are written as literate programs. To use them, you need the cweb tools ctangle and cweave that I build now.

    Since the TeX program is a pretty big file, you can not use the standard configuration even if you have ctangle and cweave already installed.

    Now download the cweb package from www.ctan.org and expand the files in the web2w directory creating the subdirectory cweb.

    Change to this subdirectory and try make. If it builds ctangle and cweave (using the preinstalled programs) skip the next step.

4. If it complains that it can not find ctangle then it's trying to bootstrap ctangle from ctangle.w without having ctangle to begin with. Try touch *.c and try make again. This time it should try to make ctangle from ctangle.c and common.c, running:

    cc -g -c -o ctangle.o ctangle.c

```
cc -g -DCWEBINPUTS="/usr/local/lib/cweb" -c common.c
cc -g -o ctangle ctangle.o common.o
```
[margin note: build ctangle and cweave]

Now you should have `ctangle`. Then building `cweave` should be no problem by running `make`.

5. Next I need to patch `ctangle.w`, `cweave.w`, and `common.w` to enlarge the settings for various parameters. Change to the `cweb` subdirectory and run the commands
   ```
   patch --verbose cweave.w  ../cweave.patch
   patch --verbose ctangle.w ../ctangle.patch
   patch --verbose common.w  ../common.patch
   make
   ```
   If you do not have the `patch` program, look at the patch files and read them as instructions how to change the settings in `ctangle.w`, `cweave.w`, and `common.w`; you can do these small changes easily with any text editor yourself.

   The final `make` should produce a new `ctangle` and `cweave` by running the old `ctangle` on the new `ctangle.w`, `cweave.w`, and `common.w`. The `cweb` directory contains change files to adapt the programs to particular operating systems and it might be a good idea to use them. On an Win32 machine, for example, you might want to write
   ```
   ./ctangle ctangle.w ctang-w32.ch
   ./ctangle cweave.w cweav-w32.ch
   ./ctangle common.w comm-w32.ch
   ```
   Then run the C compiler again as in the previous step.

6. Now you use your extra powerful `ctangle` and `cweave` from step 5, return to the `web2w` directory, and generate `ctex.c` and `ctex.tex` simply by running the commands
   ```
   cweb/ctangle ctex.w      ⇒ ctex.c
   cweb/cweave ctex.w       ⇒ ctex.tex
   ```

7. Compiling `ctex.c` is pretty easy: use the command
   ```
   cc ctex.c -lm -o ctex
   ```
   The `-lm` tells it to link in the C math library. You may add other options like `-g` or `-O3` as you like. What you have now is the virgin TeX program (also called `VIRTEX`).

8. If you have TeX on your system, you can generate the documentation with the command
   ```
   tex ctex.tex    or   pdftex ctex.tex.
   ```
   Otherwise, you will have to wait until step 16.

   Note that the above commands will need the files `ctex.idx` and `ctex.scn`. These are part of the `web2w` package and are produced as a side effect of running `cweave` on `ctex.w`.

11.2 Running TeX

9. Producing "Hello world!" with `ctex`.

   There are some differences between the plain TeX that you have generated now and the TeX that you get if you install one of the large and convenient

11.2 Running TeX

TeX distributions. First, there is no sophisticated searching for font files, formats, and tex input files (as usually provided by the kpathsea library), instead files are looked up in the current directory or in the subdirectories TeXfonts, TeXformats, and TeXinputs. Second, the plain TeX that you have now does not come with preloadable format files, you have to generate them first. So let's get started with populating the subdirectories just mentioned with the necessary files from the www.ctan.org archives.

The first file is the plain.tex file. You find it on www.ctan.org in the lib subdirectory of systems/knuth/dist/. This file defines the plain TeX format; save it to the TeXinputs subdirectory.

Now, do the same for the file hyphen.tex (same source same destination directory) containing basic hyphenation patterns.

10. Next, you need the TeX font metric files. Download the package "cm-tfm—Metric files for the Computer Modern fonts" from www.ctan.org and unpack the files in tfm.zip into the TeXfonts subdirectory.

11. Now you need to create cinitex, a special version of TeX that is able to initialize all its internal data structures and therefore does not depend on format files; instead it can be used to create format files. Special versions of ctex can be created by defining the C macros DEBUG, INIT, or STAT on the command line. So (compare step 7) run the command
    ```
    cc -DINIT ctex.c -lm -o cinitex
    ```

12. Ready? Start cinitex and see what happens. The dialog with cinitex should follow the outline below. TeX's output is shown in typewriter style, your input is shown in italics.
    ```
    This is TeX, Version 3.14159265 (HINT) (INITEX)
    **
    ```
    plain
    ```
    (TeXinputs/plain.tex Preloading the plain format:  codes,
    registers, parameters, fonts, more fonts, macros,
    math definitions, output routines,
    hyphenation (TeXinputs/hyphen.tex))
    *
    ```
    Hello world!

    ```
    *
    ```
    \end
    ```
    [1]
    Output written on plain.dvi (1 page, 224 bytes).
    Transcript written on plain.log.
    ```
    Well that's it. You should now have a file plain.dvi which you can open with any run-of-the-mill dvi-viewer.

13. To do the same with the virgin ctex program, you need a plain.fmt file which I produce next. Start cinitex again. This time your dialog should be as follows:
    ```
    This is TeX, Version 3.14159265 (HINT) (INITEX)
    **
    ```
    plain \dump
    ```
    (TeXinputs/plain.tex Preloading the plain format:  codes,
    registers, parameters, fonts, more fonts, macros,
    math definitions, output routines,
    ```

```
hyphenation (TeXinputs/hyphen.tex))
Beginning to dump on file plain.fmt
 (preloaded format=plain 1776.7.4)
1338 strings of total length 8447
4990 memory locations dumped; current usage is 110&4877
926 multiletter control sequences
\font\nullfont=nullfont
        ⋮
14707 words of font info for 50 preloaded fonts
14 hyphenation exceptions
Hyphenation trie of length 6075 has 181 ops out of 500
  181 for language 0
No pages of output.
Transcript written on plain.log
```
Now you should have a file `plain.fmt`. Move it to the `TeXformats/` subdirectory, where plain `ctex` will find it, and you are ready for the final "Hello world!" step.

14. Start the virgin `ctex` program and answer as follows:
    ```
    This is TeX, Version 3.14159265 (HINT) (no format preloaded)
    ```
    **&*plain*
    Hello world!
    \end
    ```
    [1]
    Output written on texput.dvi (1 page, 224 bytes).
    Transcript written on texput.log
    ```
    The "&" preceding "*plain*" tells TeX that this is a format file. Your dvi output is now in the `texput.dvi` file.

15. If you have `ctex.tex` from step 6, `ctex` from step 7, and `plain.fmt` from step 13, producing `ctex.dvi` using `ctex` itself seems like a snap. Running `ctex` on `ctex.tex` will, however, need the include file `cwebmac.tex` which you should have downloaded already with the `cweb` sources in step 3; copy it to the `TeXinputs/` subdirectory. Then `ctex.tex` will further need the `logo10.tfm` file from the mflogo fonts package. Download the file from the `fonts/mflogo/tfm` directory (part of the mflogo package) on www.ctan.org and place it in the `TeXfonts` subdirectory.

    Unfortunately TeX is a real big program and you need not only a super `ctangle` and `cweave`, you need also a super TeX to process it. The out-of-the box `ctex` will end with a "! TeX capacity exceeded, sorry [main memory size=30001]."

    So the next step describes how to get this super TeX.

16. Take your favorite text editor and open the file `ctex.w`. Locate the line (this should be line 397) where it says `enum {@+@!mem_max=30000@+};` and change the size to 50000. (You see how easy it is to change the code of TeX now?) It remains to run `ctangle` and `cc` to get the super `ctex`:

11.4 Generating ctex.w from tex.web

```
cweb/ctangle ctex.w
cc ctex.c -lm -o ctex
```
Now start super ctex and answer &*plain ctex*. You should get ctex.dvi

11.3 Passing the Trip Test

17. Passing the trip test is the last proof of concept!

    Download the package tex.zip from www.ctan.org which contains the files of systems/knuth/dist/tex (this is the original TEX distribution by Donald E. Knuth) and extract the files into the tex subdirectory of web2w (see also step 21 below).

    Perform all the steps described in tripman.tex in the tex subdirectory (you might want to create a dvi file with ctex before reading it) replacing "tex.web" by "ctex.w" and "tangle" by "ctangle". You should encounter no difficulties (if yes, let me know) if you observe the following hints:

    - Make a copy of ctex.w and modify the setting of constants as required by step 2 of Knuths instructions. If you have the patch program, you might want to use the file triptest.patch to get these changes.
    - After generating ctex.c from the modified ctex.w by running ctangle, compile ctex.c with the options -DINIT and -DSTAT like this:
      ```
      cc -DINIT -DSTAT ctex.c -lm -o cinitex
      ```
      Instead of setting **init** and **stats** in ctex.w, use the -D command line options.

11.4 Generating ctex.w from tex.web

18. To create ctex.w from tex.web, you need to build web2w, which is written as a literate program. So you can start building it from the file web2w.w or use the file web2w.c which comes with the web2w package. In the latter case, you can skip the next step.

19. You create web2w.c and web2w.h from web2w.w by running
    ```
    ctangle web2w.w    or    cweb/ctangle web2w.w
    ```
    Any ctangle program should work here, but it doesn't harm if you use your own ctangle created in step 5.

    I do not describe how to produce web2w.pdf from web2w.w: First, because you seem to have that file already if you are reading this, and second, because it is a much more complicated process. In addition, if you like reading on paper and prefer a nicely bound book over a mess of photocopies, you can buy this document also as a book titled "WEB to cweb"[8].

20. From web2w.c, web2w.h, web.l, and pascal.y, you get web2w by running
    ```
    flex -o web.lex.c web.l
    bison -d -v pascal.y
    cc -o web2w web2w.c web.lex.c pascal.tab.c
    ```
    The first command produces the scanner web.lex.c; the second command produces the parser in two files pascal.tab.c and pascal.tab.h. If your version of bison does not support an api prefix, you can use the option -p pp instead. The last command invokes the C compiler to create web2w.

21. Next I want to run `tex.web` through `web2w`. To obtain `tex.web` download the package `tex.zip` from `www.ctan.org` which contains the files of the original TeX distribution by Donald E. Knuth in directory `systems/knuth/dist/tex` and extract the files into the `tex` subdirectory of `web2w` (see also step 17).

22. Now I am ready to apply `web2w`. Run
    ```
    ./web2w -o tex.w tex/tex.web
    ```
    This command will produce `tex.w`, but I am not yet finished. I have to apply the patch file `ctex.patch` to get the finished `ctex.w` like this:
    ```
    patch --verbose -o ctex.w tex.w ctex.patch
    ```
    And `ctex.w` has been created.

References

[1] *Web2c: A TEX implementation*. https://tug.org/texinfohtml/web2c.html.

[2] Silvio Levy Donald E. Knuth. *The CWEB System of Structured Documentation*. Addison Wesley, 1994.

[3] C. O. Grosse-Lindemann and H. H. Nagel. Postlude to a pascal-compiler bootstrap on a decsystem-10. *Software: Practice and Experience*, 6(1):29–42, 1976.

[4] Donald E. Knuth. *The WEB system of structured documentation*. Calif. Univ. Stanford. Comput. Sci. Dept., Stanford, CA, 1983.

[5] Donald E. Knuth. *TEX: the Program*. Computers & Typesetting B. Addison-Wesley, 1986.

[6] Donald E. Knuth. *Literate Programming*. CSLI Lecture Notes Number 27. Center for the Study of Language and Information, Stanford, CA, 1992.

[7] Donald E. Knuth. *The Art of Computer Programming*. Addison Wesley, 1998.

[8] Martin Ruckert. *WEB to cweb*. 2017.

Index

Symbols

¬ 59
(26, 32
(#) 22
)   26, 32
.. 39
.dvi 47
=   22, 26
== 23
@   10
@! 40
@+ 29, 38
@/ 42
@; 42, 64
@< 21, 22, 31
@> 21, 22
@>= 21, 22
@$ 28
@d 22
@f 23
@p 22
26, 32, 33
{   10, 18, 19, 38
}   3, 10, 18, 19, 63
| 10
0.x version vi
1.y version vi

__VA_ARGS__ 79

A

abs 73
active_base 49
ADD 13, 19
add_module 21, 22
add_string 13, 14, 16
add_token 12, 13, 16, 20, 51
addop 102, 103

alfanum 35, 40
arg 44, 45
arg 98
argc 7, 76
args 98
argument list 67
argv 7, 76, 77
array 5, 54
array size v
array_type 95, 96
assign_stmt 99
assignment 4, 63, 68
AT_GREATER 22
AT_GREATER_EQ 22
ATAND 27, 88
ATAT 88
ATBACKSLASH 27, 37, 88
ATBAR 27, 88
ATCOMMA 27, 88
ATD 48, 88
ATDOLLAR 28, 30, 42, 64, 88
ATEQ 88
ATEX 27, 39, 40, 88
ATF 48, 88
ATGREATER 22, 42, 64, 88
atgreater 21, 31
ATHASH 27, 88
ATINDEX 27, 88
ATINDEX9 27, 88
ATINDEXTT 27, 88
ATLEFT 27, 38, 88
ATLESS 31, 42, 88
atless 21
ATP 23, 88
ATPLUS 27, 29, 39, 88
ATQM 27, 37, 88
ATRIGHT 27, 38, 88
ATSEMICOLON 27, 39, 65, 88

ATSLASH 27, 29, 42, 88
ATSPACE 60, 88
ATSTAR 88
ATT 27, 37, 88

B

backend vi
backslash 10
BAR 29, 87
baselength 76, 77
basename 76
basename 76, 77
BEGIN 19
begin 38
binary search tree 20
bison 5, 25, 33
bits 61–63
BOS 13
break 58, 59
break 73
break_in 73
build-in function 39

C

case 6, 32, 58
case label 58
case_element 63
case_element 100
case_label 100, 101
case_labels 100
case_list 59
case_list 100
case_stmt 100
CBREAK 58, 91, 100
CCASE 58, 59, 64, 69, 70, 91, 101
CCOLON 58, 91, 100
CEMPTY 59, 64, 65, 69, 70, 91
CHAR 28, 31, 41, 42, 45, 60, 64, 88, 98
char 52
character constant 42
CHECK 12, 15, 17, 19, 21, 26, 30, 31, 33, 36, 42, 45, 55, 60, 64, 65, 67, 69, 79
CHGID 22, 23
CHGTAG 22, 23
CHGTEXT 23
CHGTYPE 22
CHGVALUE 23
chr 73

CIGNORE 37, 50, 52, 62, 64–66, 69, 70, 91, 99, 100
`cinitex` 107
CINT 91
CINTDEF 40, 52, 91
CLABEL 50, 51, 65, 91, 99
clabel 50
CLABELN 50, 52, 91
CLOSE 87
close 68, 73
CMAIN 71, 91
CMAINEND 71, 91
column 29, 35, 38, 42
comma 35
comma 35, 40
command line 75
comment 18, 19, 27, 37
compiling 106
compound_stmt 100
condition 79
conditional_stmt 100
const 52
constant declaration 52
constants 91, 92
constdefinition 92
constdefinitions 92
conststringdefinition 92
continue 40
control sequence 4
convert_arg 45
COPY 13
copy_string 13, 14
count 49
CPROCRETURN 59, 64, 69, 71, 91, 100
CREFID 16, 45, 67, 91, 96, 102
CRETURN 64, 69–71, 91, 100
CSEMICOLON 51, 59, 60, 64–66, 88
CSTRDEF 40, 52, 91
CTAN 105
ctangle 64, 105
ctex.c 105
ctex.tex 105
CTSUBRANGE 53, 54, 62, 91
CUNION 54, 91
current_string 14
cweave 105
cweb 105
cwebmac.tex 6

Index 115

D

DBG 11, 14, 15, 19, 21, 23, 26, 27, 29–34, 36, 39, 40, 45, 46, 48, 49, 51, 53–59, 63, 65–68, 70, 71, 79
dbgarray 55, 56, 76
dbgbasic 11, 14, 15, 21, 40, 76
dbgbison 76
dbgbreak 59, 76
dbgcweb 29, 36, 48, 53, 54, 57, 58, 66–68, 71, 76
dbgexpand 23, 26, 31–33, 76
dbgflex 76
dbgfor 53, 63, 76
dbgid 23, 76
dbgjoin 34, 76
dbglink 19, 76
dbgmacro 49, 76
dbgnone 76
dbgparse 76
dbgpascal 27, 76
dbgreturn 65, 70, 76
dbgsemicolon 65, 76
dbgslash 39, 76
dbgstring 30, 45, 46, 51, 76
dbgtoken 23, 76
DBGTOKS 26, 79
DBGTREE 34, 79
dead_end 59
DEBUG 28, 107
Debug 28
debug 28
debugflags 23, 76, 79
debugging 10, 23, 28, 36, 61, 75, 79
DECsystem-10 1
DEF_MACRO 23
def_macro 23
default 59
define 28
DEFINITION 9, 10, 22
definition 22
direction 61–63
division 39
do 6, 59, 61
dotdot 39
double 39
double hashing 15
double quote 4
downto 61
DOWNTO_LOOP 61, 63

E

ε-TEX vii, 46
ebook vi
element type 55
element_type 55
ELIPSIS 20, 42, 88
ellipsis 20
else 4, 63, 64
empty statement 63
empty string 43, 47
empty_string 43, 46
empty_string_no 43, 46, 47
empty_stmt 99
end 63
end v, 25–27, 37, 60
end of file 23, 27
end_string 13, 14, 16
endif 28
ensure_dvi_open 47
entire_var 95, 98, 102
enumeration type 52
environment 32
environment 25, 26, 33
eof 73
eoln 73
EOS 13, 19
EQ 22, 64, 88
eq 15, 17, 23, 26, 30–33, 48–50
EQEQ 30, 38, 88
ERROR 11, 14, 25, 27, 31, 48, 54, 57, 60, 69, 70, 77, 79
error handling 79
error message 25, 77
erstat 73
exit 3, 40, 51, 65, 75, 79
exit_no 51, 65
expression 98–103

F

factor 103
false 35, 39, 59, 64, 69, 70, 73
fatal_error 45
fatal_error_no 45, 46
fflush 79
fheading 97
field declaration 54
field_var 102
fields 93
FILE 57

file   57
file buffer   57
file_type   93, 94
file_var   102
find_module   21, 22, 31
FIRST_PASCAL_TOKEN   26, 27, 60, 65, 89
first_string   20, 43
first_token   12, 22, 23, 33, 36
flags   79
flex   5, 9, 10
float_constant   39
float_constant_no   39
floating point division   39
fmt_file   57
fmt_no   47
following_directive   29, 38, 39
font metric file   107
fopen   77
for   5, 52, 57, 60, 61
for_ctrl   15, 62, 63
FOR_CTRL_BITS   62
FOR_CTRL_DIRECTION   62
FOR_CTRL_LINE   62
FOR_CTRL_PACK   62
FOR_CTRL_REPLACE   62, 63
for_stmt   101
formalparameters   98
formals   97, 98
FORMAT   9, 10, 23
format declaration   48
format_extension   46
format specification   23
forward declaration   67
found   27, 28, 30, 51
fprintf   27, 35, 75, 77, 79
fputc   35
fread   57
free   40
free_locals   17
free_modules   21
free_strings   14
free_symbols   15, 23
free_tokens   11
freopen   77
from   52, 54, 55, 79
frontend   vi
function   57, 68
function   95, 97
function header   68

function identifier   68
function_call   98, 103

G

generate_constant   56, 57
generating TEX   105
get   57, 73
get_sym_no   15, 16, 20, 46, 51, 70
getval   30, 31
global symbol   16, 28
globals   17
globals   91
glue_shrink   39
glue_stretch   39
goto   3, 51, 59, 65
goto_stmt   99
grammar   87
grouping   19
gubed   28

H

has_operators   49
HASH   33, 49, 50, 64, 88
hash   15
hash_str   50
hash table   15
HEAD   12, 87
Hedrick, Charles   1
help_line   45
help_line_no   45, 46
HEX   28, 31, 38, 64, 88
hexadecimal constant   28
HEXDIGIT   43
hi   54–56, 62, 63
HINT   vi
hsize   vii
hyphen.tex   107

I

iconst   93, 95, 101, 102
ID   16, 28, 39, 40, 46, 88
id   23, 44, 45, 60–63
identifier   15, 22, 28, 40
if   3, 28, 57
if_stmt   100
ifdef   28
IGN   37, 70
incomplete module name   20
INDENT   27, 39, 88

Index

index 40
index 55
index type 55
indexed_var 102
info 36
init 28, 109
`INITIAL` 9
initialization 28
input file 77
int 5, 40, 41, 61
`INT16_MAX` 54, 62, 63
`INT16_MIN` 54, 61, 63
`INT32_MAX` 54, 62
`INT32_MIN` 54
`INT8_MAX` 54, 62, 63
`INT8_MIN` 54, 61, 63
integer 39
internal node 10, 33
isalnum 35
isspace 42

J

join 33, 34

K

Knuth, Donald E. v, vii, 1, 109

L

label 50
label 65
label 99
label declaration 50
labeldecl 91, 96
labellist 91
labels 91
last_string 20
last_token 12, 19, 22, 23, 36
LaTeX vii
leaf node 10
left 19, 21, 33, 34
level 36
`lex` 9
limbo 9
line number 10
lineno 11, 12, 17, 25, 29–33, 36, 39, 40, 42, 45, 46, 48, 49, 51, 53–63, 65–68, 70, 71, 79

link 5, 6, 10, 15, 18–22, 25–27, 31–33, 43, 48, 49, 52–55, 57, 58, 60, 63, 66–70
literate programming vii, 1
`LNK` 52
lo 54–56, 62, 63
local label 51
local symbol 16, 28
localentire_var 96
localize 17
locallabeldecl 96
locallabellist 96
locals 17
locals 96, 97
localvardeclaration 96
localvardeclarations 96
localvariables 96
localvarids 96
log file 77
logfile 76, 77, 79

M

macro 25
macro declaration 48
macro definition 50
macro expansion 18, 31
macro parameter 22
main 7
main program 71
mark_for_variable 61, 62
math_spacing 46
math_spacing_no 47
`MAX_LOCALS` 17
`MAX_MODULE_TABLE` 20, 21
`MAX_NAME` 76, 77
`MAX_PPSTACK` 25, 26
max_reg_help_line 46
max_reg_help_line_no 45, 46
`MAX_STRING_MEM` 14
`MAX_SYMBOL_TABLE` 15, 16
`MAX_SYMBOLS` 15, 23
`MAX_TOKEN_MEM` 11
`MAX_WWSTACK` 18, 19
memory_word 57
`MESSAGE` 23, 79
message 79
message 25
meta-comment 37
`METACOMMENT` 27, 37, 88

MIDDLE   9, 10, 19, 22, 23
mk_logfile   76, 77
mk_pascal   76, 77
MLEFT   19, 27, 38, 49, 64, 87
module   9, 18, 20
module_cmp   20
module name   20, 25, 31, 42, 46
module_name_cmp   20, 21
module name expansion   31
module_root   21
module table   20
module_table   20, 21
mulop   103

N

NAME   9, 10, 22
name   15–17, 20, 23, 30, 40, 41, 43–46, 48, 49, 51, 55, 70, 71
new_character   3
new_null_box   1
new_string   13, 14, 16
new_symbol   15–17
new_token   11, 12, 34, 58
newline   42
next   10, 12, 20, 23, 25–34, 36–43, 48–60, 62–71, 79
NEXT_PARAM   67
NL   27, 29, 39, 42, 49, 88
NMACRO   16, 30, 40, 48, 50, 56, 60, 64, 88, 91, 93, 96, 99, 101, 103
nonterminal symbol   87
numeric macro   22, 46, 49, 50
numerical macro   30

O

obsolete   29, 32, 48, 50
obsolete   15, 30, 32, 48, 50
OCTAL   28, 31, 38, 64, 88
octal constant   28
odd   73
OMACRO   16, 32, 40, 48, 60, 64, 88
OPEN   87
open   33, 49
option   75
option   76
ord   73
ordinary macro   23, 32
others   59
output file   77

output routine   35
overflow   45, 46
overflow_no   45, 46

P

packed   93, 95
page builder   vi
PAND   38, 89, 103
PARAM   23, 88
param   50, 68
param   98
param_bit   67
param_mask   67, 68
parameter   26, 66
parameter   25, 26, 33
parameter list   66
parameterless macro   48
parametrized macro   23, 26, 32, 49
params   50
params   98
PARRAY   55, 90, 95
PARRAYFILEID   16, 90, 102
PARRAYFILETYPEID   16, 90
parse tree   33
parser   25, 87
parsing   5, 25
PASCAL   9, 10, 19, 22
Pascal   25
pascal   27, 76, 77
Pascal-H   1
pascal.tab.c   33
pascal.tab.h   33
pascal.y   11, 33, 87
pass by reference   57, 67
PASSIGN   38, 64, 69, 70, 89, 99–101
patch file   v, vi, 6, 28, 39, 47, 57, 110
PBEGIN   38, 59, 64, 69–71, 89, 91, 96, 97, 100
PCALLID   64, 67, 69, 70, 90, 98
PCASE   58, 64, 69, 70, 90, 94, 100
PCHAR   41, 90, 103
PCLOSE   66, 67, 89, 94, 97–99, 103
PCOLON   45, 51, 52, 54, 59, 64–66, 69, 90, 94–100
PCOMMA   38, 45, 49, 58, 68, 89, 91, 94–96, 98, 100
PCONST   37, 90, 92
PCONSTID   16, 31, 56, 73, 90, 93, 103
PDEFCONSTID   16, 90

Index

PDEFFUNCID 16, 90
PDEFPARAMID 16, 40, 66, 90
PDEFREFID 16, 66, 90
PDEFTYPEID 16, 40, 53, 90
PDEFTYPESUBID 16, 90
PDEFVARID 16, 40, 52–55, 90
PDIV 38, 40, 89, 103
PDO 57, 60, 61, 89, 101
PDOT 89, 91, 102, 103
PDOTDOT 39, 55, 62, 90, 93, 95
PDOWNTO 60, 89, 101
PELSE 42, 60, 64, 69, 70, 89, 100
PEND 54, 59, 63–65, 70, 71, 89, 91, 93, 96, 97, 100
PEOF 23, 28, 87
PEQ 38, 53, 89, 92, 102
PEXIT 52, 59, 64, 69, 70, 90, 91, 99
PFBEGIN 70, 71, 90
PFEND 70, 71, 90
PFILE 57, 90, 93
PFOR 60, 64, 69, 70, 89, 101
PFORWARD 37, 91, 96
PFUNCID 16, 40, 64, 69–71, 73, 90, 97, 98, 100
PFUNCTION 68, 90, 97
PGOTO 59, 64, 69, 70, 89, 99
PGREATER 89, 102
PGREATEREQ 89, 102
pheading 96, 97
PID 16, 28, 40, 45–47, 53–55, 62, 90–97, 101, 102
pid 97
PIF 38, 57, 64, 69, 70, 89, 100
PIN 90
PINTEGER 28, 30, 50, 55, 56, 90–94, 96, 99, 101, 103
PLABEL 37, 90, 91, 96
`plain.tex` 107
PLEFT 19, 27, 38, 64, 87
PLESS 89, 102
PLESSEQ 89, 102
PMACRO 16, 23, 32, 33, 39, 40, 48, 88
PMINUS 30, 31, 49, 56, 89, 93, 101–103
PMOD 38, 89, 103
PNIL 38, 89
PNOT 38, 89, 103
PNOTEQ 38, 89, 102
POF 37, 55, 58, 90, 93–95, 100
POP 19, 22, 23
POP_LEFT 19

POP_MLEFT 19
POP_NULL 19
POP_PLEFT 19
POPEN 33, 49, 66–68, 89, 94, 97–99, 103
popen 33
POR 38, 89, 103
POTHERS 59, 90, 100
pp_pop 26, 32
pp_push 26, 31–33
pp_sp 25–28, 30–33, 51
pp_stack 25–28, 30–33, 51
PPACKED 37, 91, 93
ppdebug 76
pperror 25
pplex 25–27, 32, 33
PPLUS 30, 49, 51, 56, 89, 91, 93, 96, 99, 101–103
pplval 25–27, 33
ppparse 33
PPROCEDURE 66, 90, 97
PPROCID 16, 46, 73, 90, 97, 98
PPROGRAM 37, 91
PREAL 90, 103
PRECORD 54, 90, 93
predefine 39, 46, 47, 73
predefined symbol 73
PREPEAT 59, 64, 69, 70, 89, 101
preprocessor 28
PRETURN 50–52, 64, 69, 70, 89, 99
PRETURNID 90
previous 10, 12, 23, 29, 34, 40, 45, 54–60, 62, 64, 65, 69, 70, 79
print 44, 46, 67
print_err 46
print_err_no 46
print_esc 49
print_nl 45, 46
print_nl_no 45, 46
print_no 45, 46
print_str 44, 46
print_str_no 45, 46
proc_stmt 98, 99
procedure 57, 66
procedure 95, 96
procedure call 67
procedure definition 67
procedures 91, 95
`PROGRAM` 22, 23
program 18
program 22, 33

program 91
programheading 91
prompt_file_name 45
prompt_file_name_no 45, 46
PSEMICOLON 37, 38, 52, 54, 55, 59, 60, 63–66, 69, 89, 91–100
PSET 90
PSLASH 39, 89, 103
PSQCLOSE 55, 89, 95, 102
PSQOPEN 55, 89, 95, 102
PSTAR 89, 102, 103
PSTRING 41, 44–46, 90, 92, 103
pstring_args 44, 45
pstring_assign 44, 45
PTHEN 38, 57, 89, 100
PTO 60, 61, 89, 101
PTYPE 90, 92
PTYPEBOOL 38, 90, 93
PTYPECHAR 38, 55, 56, 90, 93, 95
PTYPEINDEX 90
PTYPEINT 38, 90, 93
PTYPEREAL 38, 90, 93
PUNTIL 59, 89, 101
PUP 57, 90, 102
PUSH 19, 22, 23
PUSH_NULL 19
put 73
PVAR 37, 90, 95, 96, 98
PWHILE 57, 64, 69, 70, 89, 101
PWITH 90

R

read 73
read_ln 73
real 39
real 103
recids 94
record type 54
record_type 93, 94
recordsection 93, 94
REF_PARAM 67
regular expression 9, 13
related token 18
relop 102
remainder 40
repeat 59
repeat_stmt 101
repetitive_stmt 100, 101
replace 53, 61–63

replacement text 26, 32, 46
reserved words 40
reset 73
return v, 1, 3, 51, 65, 68–70
return 68
return type 68
return value 68
return_stmt 99, 100
rewrite 73
RIGHT 19, 38, 64, 87
right 19, 21, 33, 34
round 73
running TeX 105, 106

S

scanner 5, 9, 22, 23, 81
scanner action 13
scope 17
scope_close 17
scope_open 17
semantic value 26
semicolon 3, 4, 59, 63, 64, 66
SEQ 12, 22, 23
seq 12, 52
sequence number 10
sequenceno 11, 12, 58, 60, 79
SETVAL 31
sign 56, 57
sign 102
SIGN_BIT 67
signed_iconst 93
simple_expr 102
simple_iconst 93
simple_stmt 99
single_base 49
size 56
sizeof 57
space 35
special macro 32
stack 10, 18, 19, 22, 25, 26, 32
START_PARAM 67
stat 28
statement 99–101
statement sequence 63
statements 91, 96, 97, 99–101
statistics 28
stats 109
stderr 75, 77
stdint.h 54

Index

stmt 99
str 13, 14, 35, 41, 42
str_283 4
str_k 43, 44, 47
str_pool 4, 42, 47
str_start 4, 42, 47
strcat 77
strcmp 16, 20
STRING 20, 30, 41, 43–46, 64, 88, 98, 99, 102
string 4, 13, 18, 19, 41
string 13
string_length 13, 14
string_mem 13, 14
string pool 4, 19, 28, 42–44
string pool checksum 28, 42
strlen 20, 77
strncmp 20, 77
strncpy 77
strtol 30, 31, 76
structure type 54
structured statement 57
structured_stmt 99, 100
subrange 55, 56, 62
subrange 92–96
subrange type 5, 53, 54, 61
succumb 28
switch 6, 40, 58
SYM 16, 20, 22, 23, 28, 30–33, 40, 43–46, 48–51, 62, 65, 67, 68, 71
sym_no 16, 17, 20, 39, 43, 45–47, 51, 65, 70
SYM_PTR 16, 30, 32, 40, 41
sym_ptr 16, 17, 28, 30, 51, 55, 62, 63, 70, 71
SYMBOL 16
symbol 15, 16
symbol_hash 15, 16
symbol number 51
symbol pointer 51
symbol table 22, 67
symbol_table 15–17, 45, 46
symbols 15, 23

T

TAG 31, 36, 57–59, 69, 70, 79
tag 10–13, 15–20, 22, 23, 26–31, 33, 34, 36, 37, 39, 40, 42, 45, 46, 48–53, 55, 56, 58–60, 62–66, 68–70, 79

tag_known 27, 28
tagname 11, 23, 27, 40, 58, 79
tags 53
tail 69, 70
tail position 3, 68
tangle 1, 4, 5, 9, 19, 25
tats 28
term 102, 103
terminal symbols 87
TEX 9, 10, 19, 22
TEX_area 46
TEX_font_area 46
TEX Live 1
TeXfonts 107
TeXfonts_no 47
TeXformats 107
TeXinputs 107
TeXinputs_no 47
TEXT 13, 22, 42, 88
text 11–13, 20, 23, 29–31, 36–38, 41, 42, 52, 55, 58, 65
THE_TOKEN 19, 23, 27, 79
tini 28
to 52, 54, 55, 60, 79
TO_LOOP 61, 63
TOK 13, 19, 22, 23
TOK_RETURN 51
token 9, 10, 22, 25, 87
token_mem 11
token2string 27, 31–33, 35, 36, 42, 53, 55, 56, 63, 79
total_shrink 39
total_stretch 39
trip test v, vii, 6, 105, 109
true 16, 27, 30, 35, 39, 50, 55, 59, 60, 63, 64, 66, 69, 73
type 52
type 53
type 32
type 15, 22, 53, 55, 62, 66, 68
type 92, 94–96
type declaration 53
type identifier 53, 66
type_name 53
typedef 53
typedefinition 92
typedefinitions 92
typename 93, 94, 97, 98
types 91, 92

U

UINT16_MAX   54, 62, 63
UINT32_MAX   54
UINT8_MAX   54, 62, 63
uint8_t   61
union type   54
University of Hamburg   1
unnamed module   25
unsigned_const   103
until   59, 63
UP   54
up   10, 25, 53–55, 59, 62, 67, 68
usage   75–77
use   50

V

val   31, 44–46
value   15, 23, 30, 31, 33, 34, 44–46, 49–51, 54–57, 61, 62, 65, 67, 68, 70, 71, 79
VAR_LOOP   61
vardeclaration   95
vardeclarations   95
variable   99, 102, 103
variable declaration   52, 66
variables   91, 95
variadic macro   49
variant   94
variant part   54
variant_part   93, 94
variants   94
varids   95
varlimit   101, 102
varlist   52, 53, 55, 66
version 0.1   v
version 0.2   v
vsize   vii

W

w_file_name   76, 77
wback   64, 65
WDEBUG   29, 39, 40, 88
WEB   1, 9
web.l   9, 11, 13, 32, 81
web2w.c   7, 109
web2w.h   7, 13, 109
WEBEOF   23, 87
webmac.tex   6
wend   65

WGUBED   29, 39, 89
while   57, 59
while_stmt   101
wid   40, 52, 53, 55, 60, 66, 67, 71
win   77
WINIT   29, 40, 89
winsert_after   58, 65
wneeds_semicolon   64, 65
wprint   35–39, 43, 47, 48, 50–54, 56–60, 66, 71
wprint_to   36, 37, 48, 52–55, 57, 58, 60, 66–68
wput   29, 35, 37–44, 47–50, 52, 55, 56, 58, 66–68
wputi   35, 44, 47, 48, 56
wputs   29, 35, 37, 38, 40–44, 47, 48, 50, 52, 55, 57–60, 63, 66–68, 71
wreturn   69, 70
write   73
write_arg   98
write_ln   73
wsemicolon   64, 65
wskip_to   37, 48
WSTAT   29, 40, 89
wtail   69
WTATS   29, 89
WTINI   29, 89
wtoken   36, 37, 49, 68
ww_flex_debug   76
ww_is   18, 19
ww_pop   18, 19
ww_push   18, 19
wwin   9, 77
wwlex   9
wwlineno   11
wwout   9, 77
wwsp   18, 19
wwstack   18, 19
WWSTRING   20
wwstring   20
wwtext   13, 20

X

x_over_n   70
xclause   40
xn_over_d   70

Index

Y
yacc 25, 33
yytext 16

Z
zero_based 55

Crossreference of Sections

⟨Character k cannot be printed⟩ Defined in section 128. Used in section 127.
⟨convert some strings to macro names⟩ Defined in section 125 and 136.
    Used in section 124.
⟨convert token t to a string⟩ Defined in section 39 and 189. Used in section 99.
⟨convert NMACRO from WEB to cweb⟩ Defined in section 143. Used in section 141.
⟨convert OMACRO from WEB to cweb⟩ Defined in section 142. Used in section 141.
⟨convert PMACRO from WEB to cweb⟩ Defined in section 145. Used in section 141.
⟨convert t from WEB to cweb⟩ Defined in section 79, 80, 104, 106, 107, 108, 109, 112, 115, 116, 119, 121, 122, 123, 124, 141, 147, 154, 155, 159, 160, 161, 163, 164, 169, 170, 171, 172, 175, 178, 179, 180, 185, 191, 192, 193, 196, 197, 198, 205, 206, and 207.
    Used in section 101.
⟨count macro parameters⟩ Defined in section 144. Used in section 90.
⟨decide whether to replace a subrange type for loop control variables⟩
    Defined in section 184. Used in section 159.
⟨external declarations⟩ Defined in section 5, 6, 9, 14, 16, 17, 19, 21, 24, 25, 26, 27, 32, 38, 40, 41, 46, 48, 49, 55, 59, 60, 63, 65, 68, 83, 85, 94, 105, 130, 148, 150, 156, 162, 173, 176, 181, 183, 188, 194, 200, 202, 210, 211, 215, 216, and 217. Used in section 2.
⟨finalize token list⟩ Defined in section 66, 67, 81, 89, and 120. Used in section 4.
⟨functions⟩
    Defined in section 13, 18, 23, 31, 36, 43, 44, 47, 50, 52, 57, 58, 64, 69, 71, 72, 84, 95, 97, 99, 101, 103, 111, 118, 131, 132, 134, 149, 167, 174, 177, 182, 186, 187, 199, 201, and 209.
    Used in section 1.
⟨generate cweb output⟩ Defined in section 100 and 126. Used in section 1.
⟨generate array offset⟩ Defined in section 166. Used in section 164.
⟨generate array size⟩ Defined in section 165. Used in section 164.
⟨generate definition for string k⟩ Defined in section 129. Used in section 126.
⟨generate definitions for the first 256 strings⟩ Defined in section 127.
    Used in section 126.
⟨generate macros for some strings⟩ Defined in section 137. Used in section 129.
⟨generate string pool initializations⟩ Defined in section 140. Used in section 126.
⟨global variables⟩ Defined in section 11, 15, 20, 29, 34, 42, 45, 51, 54, 61, 70, 96, 113, 133, 138, 146, 151, 158, 195, 203, and 212. Used in section 1.
⟨initialize token list⟩ Defined in section 22, 62, 114, 135, 139, 152, 204, and 208.
    Used in section 4.
⟨internal declarations⟩
    Defined in section 3, 10, 28, 33, 53, 98, 102, 110, 117, 157, and 168. Used in section 1.

⟨ internal node ⟩   Defined in section 93.   Used in section 6.
⟨ leaf node ⟩   Defined in section 7.   Used in section 6.
⟨ open the files ⟩   Defined in section 214.   Used in section 213.
⟨ parse Pascal ⟩   Defined in section 92.   Used in section 1.
⟨ process the command line ⟩   Defined in section 213.   Used in section 1.
⟨ process the end of a code segment ⟩   Defined in section 87.   Used in section 72.
⟨ read the WEB ⟩   Defined in section 4.   Used in section 1.
⟨ show summary ⟩   Defined in section 12, 30, 35, and 56.   Used in section 1.
⟨ special treatment for WEB tokens ⟩   Defined in section 73, 74, 75, 76, 77, 78, 82, 86, 88, 90, 91, 153, and 190.   Used in section 72.
⟨ token specific info ⟩   Defined in section 8 and 37.   Used in section 7.
⟨ web2w.h ⟩   Defined in section 2.

Manufactured by Amazon.ca
Bolton, ON